To Mrs. Amazing (Amber) and The CraZies

Your love goes beyond my Human Doing and inspires me more every day on my journey toward Becoming Human

Table of Contents

Becoming Human: Introduction

Becoming Human. You may have come this far just out of curiosity over the title. You might be wondering is there really a need to write a personal development book about a process that is the result of simple biology? If ones DNA happens to organize itself in such a way to where a scientist can classify it as homo sapient, then "Voila!" The task of becoming a human being is complete. Right? There's nothing more. It's time to just get on with the doing. Grow up. Scrape a knee. Survive middle school. Get a degree. Fall in love. Face some heartache, or survive a tragedy. Change careers. Build a 401K. Retire. Buy a R.V. See the Grand Canyon. Get a disease. Pick a burial plot. Call it a life. That's it. Right?

In our modern world the doing part of human seems to be the point. Our children's childhoods are planned and structured for maximum effectiveness, and our vacations are loaded with an agenda that would have made Napoleon's march to Moscow feel, well, like vacation. The being part of human seems a mere biological construct. We were created a little more sophisticated than other mammals. Prescribed bigger brains so we could figure out how to put a man on the moon and a rover on Mars.

Given an opposable thumb so we could dominate and throw a mean fastball. Being human it seems isn't about being at all. It's about doing.

When our transformation from human being into human doing actually begins is hard to nail down. It probably begins not too long after we move from the cozy little bubble of our mommy's tummy to the cold sterilized atmosphere of the delivery room. It's not really our fault it seems, it's just the way things happen. After a few "ew's, ah's, and coochie coos" the first words we actually begin hearing the adults around us utter are things like, "Oh, look! She opened her eyes!" and "He can already hold his head up on his own." Beyond whether we look more like mom or dad, there is little people notice about who we are. Most of how we're identified from the beginning is by what we can do. This is compounded throughout the rest of our lives as we develop particular interest and choose our hobbies, careers, and even life's relationships based in large part on what they can do for us and what we can do for them.

Our being has been broken, because of the disease of our doing.

***

Jesus said, "Unless you become like little children you will never get into the Kingdom of Heaven."

Now, don't give up on the book just because I introduce one who has become synonymous as a religious figure head. It's not his fault. He never intended for his words and teachings to be misused and abused the way they have been throughout history. That's on the folks who missed his point due to using the ears of their ego versus listening with their heart. Jesus never intended a message of condemnation or exclusivity. His intention was an invitation into a gathering of others who too were devoted to a life centered in love and community beginning with himself. He called it the Kingdom of God. That's the Jesus I see when I read the accounts of his life in the New Testament, it's the Jesus whom I have experienced, and it's the Jesus I will refer to many times throughout this book, so just giving you a heads up. You are gonna fall in love with him and his message, if you give him a fair shot. Listen with your heart.

Back to Jesus statement, "Unless you become like little children you will never get into the Kingdom of Heaven."

Jesus' life and teachings are filled with all kinds of mysteriousness. His above statement stereotypically exemplifies his penchant toward enigma. What's the Kingdom of Heaven and why would one want to get into it? Also, how would a full blown adult become like a child? Isn't the whole point to grow up and become independent? A good citizen and contributing member of society? Become one that does stuff? What age child must one become to get into this mysterious kingdom? Is it a child as young as two or as old as eleven? So much craziness in this one little statement! And one of the problems is that we haven't read this whole book yet, so more than likely we are approaching these mysteries with our doing mind which only further confounds and confuses.

While all of these questions deserve consideration, and for some of them we will provide answers, the easier one to resolve is "What age child must one become to get into this mysterious kingdom?" A kingdom I would argue is for human beings. A kingdom where you can leave your doing at the gate, because it's not necessary as a self identification piece like it is in our current culture. What age must you be?

Jesus answers this in an encounter with a religious leader of his day named Nicodemus. One evening under the cover of dark Nicodemus shows up because he too has been intrigued by Jesus. He wants to pay him a quick compliment, but obviously doesn't want all his religious buddies to know about it. Thus, coming to see Jesus after dark.

Nicodemus says, "Jesus, I just want you to know that I have been paying close attention to you. I'm convinced that you are the real deal, and that God has sent you. Nobody would be able to do the miraculous things you have done, if God wasn't the one that had sent them."

Please note what it is that Nicodemus had noticed about Jesus. The things that Jesus had been doing. He had been observing the miracles of Jesus and not his motives. This is typical of we human doings. It's what this whole book is trying to help us get over. Rarely do we take the time to look deeply into the eyes and soul of another in order to identify who they really are. We can spend half a lifetime lying in bed next to someone and never really discover what makes them tick. As long as their doing is meeting our need, then their life mission is accomplished in our eyes. We watch other's actions and determine who they are accordingly. And if it's not bad enough that we determine who others are by their doing, then it is an absolute atrocity that we look in the mirror and do it to ourselves. I do, therefore I am, is an unfortunate and empty way of living.

Jesus' answer to Nicodemus question was simple, "You must be born again."

That's the answer to our question too. The question of what age child do we have to become to get back to our original selves? The question of how do we stop the madness of all this doing and become human beings?

We must go back to the beginning and start all over again. We must be born again. We must become human.

How do we do this? Well, I'm glad you asked. Keep reading...

The Wake Up Call

Actually, my wake up call and invitation to rebirth came in the form of a text. I was lying in bed watching a movie when I got the now infamous text. It was from my pastor, who also happened to be my boss.

> Pastor: Hey pastor—what's your schedule today? I need to meet with you for a bit. Wd you be free around 12:30?
>
> Me: I can be there around 12:30. Everything okay?
>
> Pastor: Will be!
>
> Me: See you at 12:30.

Everything about this impromptu request for a meeting felt wrong. This was Friday, and it was our day off. If this was the typical pastoral emergency, then he would have just told me over the phone. If it was something that had to do with one of our staff, then he would have at least given me a heads up as to what I was walking into. Nothing normal was happening here. My greatest fear was emerging from the dark recesses of my doing mind. A fear that had visited me on a daily basis for about nine years, but that I had always been able to put back in its mental compartment without it completely taking over, or becoming reality. Now it felt as if it would not be subdued. It was going to finally have its day. The muscles all around my torso felt like they were contracting. It was as if the breath that I relied on for life was being extinguished from my lungs and as I grasped for it, my fingers just slipped right through. At this rate I wouldn't even be able to make it to the meeting because my emotional heart already felt like it was giving out. All of this panic—that I feel even now as I write about this episode again—was pointing to the fact that maybe I had been found out.

I was lying in bed watching a movie when I received the text. This was not a completely abnormal Friday morning routine for me, since it was my day off. Back then I wasn't spending my down time writing this book, or in the gym working on my nonexistent physique like I do now. I was in bed watching a movie with a cold one. Yes, I said "cold one." No, I'm not talking about an ice pack—remember I never went to the gym—or a coke. I am talking about a beer. I will now pause and give you a moment to put a few things together and make sure you're still following me.

Yes, it was morning. Yes, I said beer. Yes, I have worked for a church for most of my career as a pastor and I was a pastor's kid. Yes, I was a pastor having a cold beer in the morning on my day off. Actually, let's get a little more honest than that. I would have multiple beers before that day was through. In total transparency, I had multiple alcoholic drinks before everyday was through. Why? I am an alcoholic!

Alcoholism is one of two diseases that I posses. Yes, alcoholism is a disease. If we put my head in a magnetic resonance imaging machine—you probably know that better by its street name of M.R.I.—and put your head in the same machine, then somebody gave us both an alcoholic beverage—assuming you're not also an alcoholic—your brain would say something like, "That's nice." Mine would light up like a firecracker on Independence Day!

The second disease that I posses is that of human doing. In fact, this is my baseline disease that helped to fuel my disease of alcoholism. This is not a judgmental statement at all, but you probably have it too. It's probably the fuel of your own hated habits like ambitious spending, extra dessert, selfish sex, over-booked calendar, and general emotional malaise. I've met very few humans who have come to the awareness that they have such a disease, and even fewer who have actually overcome it. Most of us who become aware of the disease's control over our life usually experience some kind of wake up call. For some it is more dramatic than others, and on this particular Friday mine was feeling like a version of Hamlet produced by George Lucas.

As you could surmise I wouldn't be finishing my movie, or my beer for that matter. It was time to shower, get ready, brush my teeth three times, gargle lots of mouthwash in hopes of masking the brewery smell exuding from my lungs, and onto discovering whatever it was that this suddenly urgent meeting had in store. Had I been found out? My mind was spinning with potential topics. Being a naturally anxious individual who can forecast the worst in any situation wasn't really helping. My mind was caught in full-on doing mode. I tried to tell myself the best like, *in ministry life it really could be anything,* but in reality I already knew what was up before I even arrived at the church building.

Walking up the stairs to my pastor's office for this *"Is everything okay? It will be meeting."* was like a slow slog through a marshy swamp. With each step the weight of my legs felt heavier. I wasn't entirely sure if it was the result of what had come to be the physical effects of my everyday morning hangover that was getting to me, or if it was carrying the weight of the enormous guilt and fear that hung over my heart like an oversized ornament on a wimpy Charlie Brown Christmas tree. Whatever it was, it was turning this little trek up a small flight of stairs into a hike up Everest with a two hundred and fifty pound pack and no climbing gear. Every step came with great effort and at an emotional cost.

At that moment my addicted doing brain felt there was a plus side of this strenuous, time-slowing climb. It gave me a couple of added seconds of doing, and a further chance to plan my "evade and escape." Should this meeting be anywhere close to the subject matter I was suspecting, centering around my obsessive predilection toward alcohol, then in these brief moments I was trying to finalize what my approach to "you're caught" would be. Maybe, I'd throw out the, "I'm really tired and bordering on burnout" card. Or, there was the, "I've been really sick the last couple of days, and I think it's time I go to the doctor. Please pray for me." One line that was always boiling away under the surface was, "Forget you! How dare you accuse me of such a thing! You can take this job and shove it!" With that one I probably would have thrown in a few expletives for good effect and kicked over a chair on the way out to the unemployment line. Then again, there was the classic statement of denial and deflection, "I don't know what you're talking about. Are you sure you're okay?" Please note my addicted human doing brain never contemplated this as an opportunity to just tell the truth. That was never going to be an option. If I did, I would have to deal with what had turned me into a human doing in the first place, and my ego would be having none of that. Told you it was a long slow walk up those stairs.

I knocked and then slowly peaked my head in the office door. My pastor ushered me in. Little did I realize that the sound of the door clicking shut behind me was the sound that would come to represent the closing of one of the most painful chapters in my life. The chapter on active addiction and human doing. At that moment, it sounded more like the closing of a cell door on my future.

My pastor is one of the closest living examples of Jesus that one may ever get to meet. I mean that sincerely. He is most humble, gentle and kind, but he is also always willing to have a crucial conversation, if necessary. He typically has a very inviting presence about him, but that wasn't the case on this day. I have rarely been on the receiving end of a crucial conversation from him, but on this day it would certainly be different. On this day, I would be in the most crucial conversation of my life. I knew it the moment I saw him. Today was going to be all business. Even as I write this, I can feel my heart playing a rapid rhythm in my chest. The same beat it was playing the day I walked into that office. My defenses were up immediately. This was game on. I had an addiction to protect, and a doing to defend.

He was already sitting in his normal spot at the head of his kitchen table turned office furniture. Don't doubt it. It actually works. He was leaned back in his chair, and this obviously meant we were going to go ahead and forgo our usual initial meeting niceties which include the man hug–hand shake with the lean in shoulder bump and wrap around back tap with the free hand. Nope. Today, I just sat down.

"John, have you been drinking again?" he asked.

Well, that answered that. I knew what this meeting was going to be about. I had been mentally preparing all morning for this moment. Heck, I had been mentally preparing for a moment like this for years. The daily life of an alcoholic is constant preparation for moments like these. *What am I going to say if that officer behind me turns on his blue lights and pulls me over? What's my response to my chiropractor should he mention the alcohol he smells on my breath every time I come in for an adjustment? How will I explain the empty bottle of vodka to my wife, if she finds it before I am able to secretly throw it away in someone else's trash can? How do I describe to my doctor the way I think I got the massive gash in my ear while sleeping?* (More on that interesting incident a bit later). And, of course, the kicker I was being confronted with now, coming from my boss, *"John, have you been drinking again?"*

In spite of all the years of mental, emotional, and spiritually exhausting preparation for a moment just like this, somehow

I was still caught off guard. How could that be? I had even reviewed all the possibilities on the way up the stairs. I had positioned myself at the perfect distance from the table and from where my pastor was sitting just so he wouldn't smell the beer on my breath from the party I was throwing myself before he had so rudely interrupted me with a text requesting this meeting. I was ready! But, now having been asked the question, it turns out I wasn't. My response revealed that all of my preparation had failed.

"No, I haven't," I lied.

***

The old cliché is that the first step to getting help for a problem is admitting that you have one. It's a true statement, but the part I hadn't ever realized is that you have to take the step after that, and then the one after that. Six years earlier I was willing to admit that I had a problem. I had at least admitted it to myself as well as my wife—as if she didn't already know I had a problem before I verbally said it to her. We human doings think we are good at hiding the things we've been doing that we're not proud of. We're not. I had wanted off of this crazy train of drinking and some peace from all the doing for a long time. I had been a "do"-aholic ever since my wife had known me, and then a few years into our marriage had compounded my first disease with the second of alcoholism. Drinking felt like the only way I could calm the incessant need for accomplishing, achieving, winning, and doing. My brain was always on the go. I couldn't watch a T.V. show, be present in a conversation with my children, or try and go to sleep without the incessant churning of my mind. It seemed only a few good drinks could slow it down and ease the accompanying anxiety of all that kinetic mental energy. But now that I could admit that alcohol was a problem, how does a pastor get off this crazy train without losing everything?

One day, probably not long after coming clean to myself about my alcoholism, I was watching an episode of the A&E

television series "Intervention." I'm not exactly sure why I had chosen to watch such a show in my condition, except that it was my only real source for an inside look as to how one might go about getting some help. As this particular episode was coming to an end I was so incredibly frustrated. The protagonist in this plot was a young man who seemed to have one of the most remarkable support systems in the world. Here he was sitting in the middle of a couch surrounded by friends and family. All of them were willing to do anything they needed in order to help him find freedom. His employer was even there offering support.

His whole story seemed to be in deep contrast to mine. The story I had written about myself was that should I even find one soul to tell outside of my bride, then they would blast it on social media that night, tag me in it, my deacons would read my feed—I was actually the Lead Pastor of another church at the time and social media was one of the ways the oldest deacon was able to keep an eye on me—and then would come church business meetings, enough severance to pay my final month's electric bill at the parsonage, unemployment due to the scarlet letter tattooed on my chest, bankruptcy—I was almost there anyways—and ultimately me and my family living under a bridge in East Baltimore, where I would likely make it only a few nights before I caught the Ebola virus and became a cadaver at the nearest medical school. Yes, I am aware that we don't have Ebola here, but when I'm thinking of the worst that can happen, I go for the gold.

All this kid on the show had to do was get on a plane and go to rehab. And, he wouldn't do it!

I was so mad. I was virtually yelling at the T.V. Not really in an effort to save this young man's life, but more out of anger and envy that someone could have such a chance to get off the crazy train of addiction and not do it. *I wanted that chance.* All I could do was yell, "Get on the damn plane! Please, go get on the damn plane!" I vowed that day sitting on my couch that if I ever got the chance to get on the plane, I would do it.

Five years went by. This was five years of always wondering if somebody wanting to talk to me meant that I had been found out. Five years of waking up most mornings at around 2:30 AM and not being able to go back to sleep because the effects of the alcohol were wearing off. Five years of making sure we could pay all the bills and there would be enough left over to keep me drinking at the necessary addictive levels. Five years of isolating myself, sometimes physically and always emotionally, so that no one could figure out the secret that I was keeping. Five years of physical deterioration at a time in my life when I should have been enjoying my physical prime. Five years of non-stop doing and believing that if I could just finally get to where I thought I should be in life, then this little issue with alcohol would self correct. Five more years of drinking. Five more years of hell.

It was now one year before my most crucial conversation with my pastor, and the invitation to rebirth. It was only a few weeks before the kids got out of school to begin the summer and I had one of those days that largely consisted of sitting in my office in meeting after meeting after meeting. Who am I kidding? That's almost every day for me. About half way through the day I noticed that my lower back was starting to hurt. This was nothing new, lower back issues have long been one of my many physical ailments. This ailment was real and not like most of my others, which during my active addiction were due to my self-diagnosed hypochondria.

Over the course of the next few days the pain began to grow at an enormous rate. I had dealt with back pain before, but this was becoming much worse and more chronic than anything previous. As a few weeks drug on, and while it was already putting a very negative spin on what was planned to be an epic summer, it slowly began to make its way into my hip area. A trip to my chiropractor didn't do anything to help. I take that back. It did help to accentuate my hypochondria. He commented on a few other symptoms that I was experiencing and before I knew it I was seeing Dr. Google asking about words like "colon" and "cancer". I was full on convinced that all these years of abusing my body with do, do, do, and daily ingesting a chemical that is used in most cleaning agents had run its course. Even if I was to quit drinking now, it was probably too late. If it wasn't colon cancer that had metastasized into my hip, then surely my liver was on the brink of giving up, and if that didn't get me then I knew my blood pressure was on the outer limits. My last couple of trips to a patient care facility—usually after a night of sustained intoxication—had revealed crazy high blood pressure for which I then received blood tests to ensure that my kidneys had not disintegrated.

Most normal people would visit a doctor at this point. But then again, I wasn't normal, because most normal people don't drink copious amounts of alcohol a day either. In my mind visiting a doctor would only confirm what I already suspected, that it was too late. That I was going to die as a result of all my drinking. I addictively, and thus fearfully, reasoned that it would be better to let whatever disease or illness progress until it either killed me instantly, or I was so sick that when it was discovered how I had gotten that way people would just feel sorry for me instead of judge me. As the Russian said of Apollo Creed in Rocky IV, "If he dies, he dies." My fear was so confounding at this point that death was what I would accept, not the exposure of my addiction.

There was one thing standing in the way of calling it a life, my three Crazies. I couldn't imagine them having to grow up without a dad. I had reasoned that my beautiful wife could easily find another man to love. A man that carried with him fewer flaws and the ability to navigate life without the aid of mind altering substances, but my Crazies could never find another dad. To lose a parent as a child is devastating enough without the complicating story of losing one to a complex yet senseless addiction. In rare moments of clarity I was able to imagine being around for a potential future where I watched my oldest try out for the varsity basketball team, where my middle son launched his own business as a young high school entrepreneur, and where I cheered as my little girl graduated from my college alma mater and I walk her down the aisle and into the arms of Mr. Right. None of this required that I DO anything. It would require that I BE around. And being around would require that I be reborn.

So here I was, a year away from real recovery and undergoing rebirth from human doing into human being, on a hot Sunday afternoon in July, in pain that made lying down, sitting, standing, and walking miserable. Lost in the blinding darkness of addiction. Having come to the sincere conclusion that I would never see the day when I would walk my five-year-old Lady Liberty down the aisle. And then came the text. This one was from my best friend and fellow pastor Tally Wilgis. It was the title and link to an article.

"Perry Noble removed as pastor at New Spring for personal behavior related to alcohol." (thestate.com)

As I clicked on and read about how one of America's most prominent and influential pastors, one for whom I had personally developed a great deal of respect, had come to a point in his own life where alcohol had taken over, I began to realize that this story was not just about him. It was about me. I was reading what would be my own reality in the very near future. Soon it would all be gone.

Unless?

At that moment I made the most important phone call that I have ever made in my life. I called my friend who had just sent me the text. While a couple of encounters in recent times had led him to believe that there might be something unhealthy in my relationship with alcohol, he was largely unsuspecting of my confession which would follow. The confession that opened the portal to what would be a long, arduous, and messy rebirth into Becoming Human.

Over the course of the next few weeks and months to follow I began to dip my toes into the waters of recovery. What this meant was that I began to see a professional counselor, attend a few meetings designed for people like me who have a problem with alcohol, tell my pastor I had an issue with the substance, and not drink quite as much, thus attempting to fool myself and the less than a handful of people who knew that I was working on it, that I was getting better. I would later discover that doing it half way is classic addictive, and thus human doing, behavior. You don't transform from a human doing to a human being by doing a few more or new things. You can't be partially reborn. It's an all-or-nothing scenario. Your life depends on it.

A year had passed and dipping my toes and partial rebirth weren't working. As my disease progressed my daily intake of alcohol was on the uptake. I was still all doing and no being. That became obvious when here I was sitting in my boss's office and he asked me if I was drinking again and I lied.

We talked longer. He worked the question several different ways. Finally, he asked me if I had a drink at any time since my initial admission of guilt to him a year ago. For some reason I felt safe enough in that moment to at least fess up to that. I wouldn't confess that I had been drinking that morning, or over the last few days leading up to this moment, but any time within the last year? Sure, why not?

I said, "Yes, I have drank in the last year."

At that moment he simply said, "Then it's time for us to get you some help."

This was my moment to have a chance to get on that plane. To leave behind a life that wasn't working. To walk away, not only from alcohol, but from the deeper lie that I had come to believe about myself. The lie that every person falls prey to at some point in their early existence. The lie that my identity was found in all of my accomplishments and failures. The lie that I was nothing more than a human doing. Breathing oxygen for no other reason than to please others, accomplish stuff, and attempt to be remembered for something I had done in my few brief moments on the planet. This moment offered a way out of all of that, an authentic rebirth, a genuine do over, a chance for Becoming Human.

In the few moments that followed my partial admission in that office, I told my pastor the story of watching that episode of Intervention. As I was getting ready to depart, his demeanor had softened. He gave me a hug.

He said, "John, I think it's time to go get on the plane."

I said, "Yes, sir. I will."

I did. I began the journey from human doing to human being. What follows are a few important things I learned along the way. I hope they're going to do as much for you as they have for me.

Defining FEAR the Right Way

It was an early morning after yet another late night of pounding back the beer. I was about seven years into this active addiction and by this time there were few nights that did not end late, with my body having received all the alcohol it was going to absorb, and then shutting down into the unproductive sleep-state known as passing out. As you can probably imagine, this made for some very unpleasant morning experiences. Awakening in a much groggier than normal way, like one who is just emerging from anesthesia after a major surgery. Immediately feeling the deep ache and subsequent gag reflex brought on by what was now the ever present state of constant nausea from the initial stages of withdrawal, and then spending a few moments trying to recollect any arguments that I might have had, or stupid things I'm might have done, as the result of my previous day of intoxication.

On the morning of this Greek tragedy, I was enjoying all the pleasantries mentioned above with one little added bonus. As I awoke I noticed that my ear felt a little weird. It wasn't anything painful, but I also knew quickly that there was something that wasn't normal. I begrudgingly staggered my way out of bed and into the bathroom. I looked in the mirror and there was my morning surprise! Right there on my right tragus was this massive, perfectly sliced gash. In case you haven't already Googled it, the tragus is that weird rounded mountain top on the outer portion of the ear protecting the entrance to the external auditory canal–the tunnel that carries sound waves down to your ear drum. It had a gash! Nothing gross, because it looked like it had been done by a well calculated surgeon's hand. And while it also didn't hurt, my best inner diagnostician knew that it shouldn't be allowed to just stay that way. This thing was going to need stitches. Stitches would mean doctors, and doctors would mean nurses, and nurses would mean blood pressure tests, and blood pressure tests would mean stories I would have to make up as to why mine was probably going to be so high, not to mention the story I was going to have to tell as to how I had received this special gape in my ear. At this point, I considered channeling my inner survivalist Navy SEAL and doing it myself, but then I realized I'm not much on channeling, and even if I was, I don't have an inner survivalist Navy SEAL. Nope. I was going to have to break down and do what I had vowed well over two years earlier not to do. Go to the doctor when I had been drinking.

You see the last two times I had been to the doctor's office for something as simple as the common cold or viral infection things had gone awry in my little addicted, human doing brain. I would go in simply hoping to get a prescription that would knock out the congestion and quell the cough. After doing the paperwork and then reading all 587,287 words of Tolstoy's "War and Peace" during the obligatory extended stay in the waiting room, the nurse would call me back and I would enter the domain of the dreaded arm crushing, fear inducing sphygmomanometer. Using the technical name of the device sounds way more intimidating than telling you that I was just having my blood pressure checked. In these moments the sphygmomanometer came to represent much more than a calculation as to where my blood pressure currently resided.

This device for me was more like a polygraph machine that threatened my secret, and to expose my secret was my deepest misdefined fear.

One of the many health issues of an alcoholic is that of high blood pressure. Blood pressure really has a tendency to hike up there when you are going through withdrawals or after having made a night of it on the town. I had first discovered this when I was applying for some term life insurance. I had abstained from eating or drinking since after midnight as they had suggested, but it was the binger before midnight that fouled up all the medical test, that were necessary for the term life insurance application the next morning. Since discovering this was a thing, I had a certain disdain for this part of a visit to the doctor. It meant the doctor was going to eventually ask me about my lifestyle choices, and in my particular position, I didn't even trust the world of doctor-patient confidentiality. My secret was my secret and that's where it was going to stay. I felt that I could trust no one. Couple this with the whole notion of "white coat syndrome" where the patient's blood pressure goes up just because they are nervous about having it taken in the first place, and you can imagine my readings were way North of Santa's home base. On this particular gashed ear visit to the doctor they were sky rocketing toward Andromeda.

The nurses seemed to think that sewing up my ear was the least important thing at the moment, because what good is a whole ear if you stroke out and can't use it. They kindly asked me to walk back to an examination room, take off my shirt, and lie back on the table. Within a few short minutes they had wheeled in yet another machine. What appeared to me to be an even more elaborate version of a polygraph, but this was called an electrocardiogram or EKG. Moments later I had nodules stuck all over me that were attached to wires leading back to this nefarious device. Not long thereafter blood was being confiscated from my veins so they could run test on the functionality of my kidneys. I was laying there in absolute terror.

The dialogue in my head was a cacophony of shame and judgment mixed with just the right amount of resentment and dread. It sounded like the cross between a judge declaring a final ruling and unappealable sentence on one who had chosen to be a serial idiot, and a man who was sharing his last words before facing the executioner.

So, this is how it all ends. This is how I was found out. Wake up with a gash in my ear from causes that I can only speculate, go to the doctor, and end up in the emergency room having broken the world record for high blood pressure. I AM SUCH AN IDIOT! I was given so many chances to DO more than this. Now everybody is going to know just how much of a loser I am. All these years of molding an image wasted. Once all of this comes out and they diagnosis me with cirrhosis of the liver it will be a long decent into death. No one is even going to be willing to come to my funeral.

And on and on and on I droned.

My most basic instinct was to detach myself from the electronic invaders and flee this terrible predicament like the cartoon of Jerry with Tom in hot pursuit. This was one of those drop-in clinics, so the only thing standing in the way of me and my car was a curtain, a few white coats—who would be so shocked by a shirtless man running and screaming like a banshee that they would surely be frozen in astonishment and unable to recapture their most recent lab rat—and the glass door in the lobby. Once I made it to my car, Baltimore-Washington International Airport was only ten minutes away. My plan was to buy a cheap ticket to somewhere in the Bahamas, so the fact that I was shirtless would make all the sense in the world to airport security. From down there I would drink my way into homelessness—which with my bank account, and having just purchased a last minute plane ticket, would take about twelve hours—but I would be homeless on the beach in the Bahamas. How bad could it really be?

The only way I knew how to define fear was Forget Everything And Run.

***

It's such a simple word, but so very easy to misdefine. In fact, it may be the most misunderstood word in the English language. Probably in every other language too, even if in other languages its mis-definition doesn't create a perfect acronym. Human doings don't like hard, we don't like pain, and we certainly don't like things that threaten our physical existence. We are hard wired within the part of our brain called the amygdala for what psychologist have come to refer to as the "fight or flight" response. If it scares us, or can potentially hurt us, then we'll either look for a way to annihilate it, or we'll take off running from it like a shirtless guy facing a bad diagnosis in an out patient clinic. Unless you can in fact channel an inner Navy SEAL, then most of us in modern society seem programmed to run from the things that scare us.

Running looks different for all of us. For some, it's scrolling through Amazon buying all kinds of unneeded items and gadgets with a "forget the credit card bill" attitude. For others, its mindlessly sitting in front of the machine with all the pretty lights, feeding it with money, endlessly hitting the button, believing that at any moment bells and whistles will sound indicating that you're instantaneously rich and all your financial woes have disappeared from inside a dark dungeon called a casino. It may be being awakened in the middle of the night because the demands of your career have entered your nightmares and you go to the kitchen to finish off the two-thirds of a chocolate cake that's left in the fridge–I like my cake cold. Running may be as devastating as believing that if you can sleep with that attractive co-worker instead of your spouse, then your monster can't reach you in their arms. Running looks different for all of us, but all human doings run.

I started running from my fears as a junior in high school. Up and until that point in my life things had gone pretty well, and I never had too many things of which to be afraid. I grew up in a loving family with a lot of parental support. I was a good student who had done pretty well in every sport in which I had participated. Friends came rather easily for me. Life was good—until young love entered the picture.

Now I'm not going to name any names because there's a good chance she's going to read this book, but I will say she was gorgeous. Surely, she won't mind that. I had been chasing her since the very first day of high school. Over the course of some letter writing—that use to be a thing—while I was away for the summer working at a camping ministry, it seemed all my chasing was finally paying off. Maybe, just maybe, I had a chance to win this young lady over. I got back from the summer and school began. All seemed to be going well until one day when I got the call from her friend telling me that she wasn't quite as into me as I had expected. This led to me writing her the longest letter yet, and then her quickly returned Post-it note affirming all my worst fears. Whatever she had thought of me before was now gone. For the first real time in my life my heart was broken. I had never really felt that type of pain before. The type of pain that is rejection. The type of pain that is someone saying, "You're not for me. I think I'll have another." Ouch!

I get it. Many of you have experienced way worse than a broken high school heart by the time you were my age in this story. Some of you have experienced rejection from a mom or dad who left you, or maybe even worse from a mom or dad who abused you. You have had your heart torn out by the sudden loss of a loved one, or you have been ridiculed, left out, and bullied because of appearance or even race. There are way worse pain invoking realities than the weak excuse of losing the girl that I came up with to begin my run. Nonetheless, it still hurt. That night I decided to Forget Everything And Run.

I had three close friends that I had been hanging with since middle school. If you have seen the movie "Stand By Me", then you get the picture. The afternoon that I had received the devastating news of love lost, I had them all come over to my place after school. It was a Friday. A couple of the guys had strayed away from our tight knit group from time to time and had tasted a little of the wilder side of life. It was from them that I wanted to get some advice. What advice was I looking for?

"Guys, how much money does it take to get some beer, and where do we go to get it?"

Up and until this point in life I had been a vocal and proud advocate of my faith in Jesus. My nickname on the high school basketball team was Reverend. How much more cliché can you get? My general and very naive take on faith was that if I did what I was supposed to, then God would do what He was supposed to, and make my life easy and good. The natural Aristotelian logic from that belief was that if I had lived in such a way as to earn the nickname Reverend, then God should do his part and grant me the girl. If that's not how life was going to work, then forget God! In my childish rebellion I decided I would show God once and for all what I thought about Him not allowing things to work out according to my dictates. I would do the thing that I had been led to believe through some immature and misplaced theology was the thing that would get back at God the most. I would go drink beer! It seems silly now, but it was the best my seventeen year old broken heart could come up with in the face of the pain it was feeling.

That was the night I drank my first six pack. The problem is I liked it. I liked it a lot. I also acquired a pair of emotional running shoes. I learned on that night that if there was anything that hurt, anything that caused me emotional harm, anything of which I was afraid, all I had to do was put on my pair of running shoes called alcohol and get as fast and far away as I possibly could from whatever was causing the discomfort. Throughout my teenage and young adult years I would use these shoes sparingly, but as I got older and life got increasingly more complicated, with way bigger monsters, I used those shoes more and more. Like Forest Gump, I would end up running and running having even lost awareness of why and from what I was running. I ran continuously for nine years.

Just curious. When did you pick up your running shoes? When did you begin to believe the false definition of FEAR– Forget Everything And Run? For most of us it probably was during childhood, or those ever important and often turbulent teen years. Perhaps you were fortunate enough to put off any major emotional harms until young adulthood. But no matter, life at some point hit you smack in the face. It hurt. Maybe it still hurts. A human doing's response is to DO something about it. To put on our running shoes and get as far and fast away from the pain as our little habits and addictions will allow. That's what I did, and you probably would not have picked up a book about Becoming Human if you had not either.

The first step in stopping and unlacing those running shoes involves naming the pain. Being still long enough to identify what it is you are really trying to escape. Human doings have come to believe that they are unloved for some reason. They have adopted the false belief that by doing something they can either numb the pain or win the love they so desperately crave by doing. What persons or circumstances caused the pain that caused you to put on those particular running shoes? What brand of running shoes are you wearing–meaning what are you using to kill the pain of feeling unloved?

Take a moment to sort this out. In fact, take as long as is necessary. If you need to make an appointment with the faith leader in your life, or schedule a coffee with a friend to get to the bottom of this, then do it. If it means finally setting an appointment with that counselor that your significant other suggested to you a few months back, then stop procrastinating and making excuses that you don't have time. At this stage in your journey naming your monster is the only thing you really do have time for, if your intention is to actually get better, feel better, BE better. Stop here. Don't even finish this chapter until you have stopped and unlaced those shoes. It's time to learn to define fear the right way, and the first step is to know what you're so afraid of, and the unhealthy ways you are dealing with it. Go for it. I'll wait.

Taking the time to do what you just did is daunting. Naming your fear and brand of running shoes is the right start. But it is just that. It is only a start. Too many people I have had the chance to encounter over the years have no problem naming what events and people of their past have caused them their emotional harm. They are more than happy to share with you their painful experience and ask you to join them in their self-destructive run toward the finish line of oblivion; or they just sit in their pain and whine. That's not what we are doing here. We are going to learn how to define FEAR like a human being does. We are going to Face Everything And Recover.

***

Growing up with my dad as a pastor meant that from early on I was well versed in all things concerning the Bible. Most of all I loved the Old Testament stories. Now I realize that's where most conscientious objectors of scripture seem to get all hung up. There is quite a bit of violence and mayhem that occurs throughout the Old Testament, and if one does not take the time to really see what's culturally going on in those stories, then it's pretty easy to mischaracterize the God, who on the surface, would seem at times to condone and even support such poor human doing behavior. However, for a boy it was exactly those objectionable portions that made the stories so mesmerizing. They even happen to carry within them some poignant reminders and practices for dealing with real life stuff. If I had paid closer attention to my favorite story of them all, then I may have learned how to properly define FEAR a lot earlier.

Reader of the Bible or not, it's a story that one really can't grow up in western culture and not have at least heard referenced at some point. It's the story of a boy named David who had to decide how he was going to define FEAR. It is found in 1 Samuel 17 in case you ever want to give it a look-see.

David was the youngest in his band of eight brothers. This meant when his older brothers were out having all the ancient masochistic fun of going to war, that David got the job of boring grunt work. David was the default shepherd of the crew. His days were spent finding sheep the best places to graze, water to drink, staying aware of impending predators, and practicing his slingshot skills for when those roaming beast made their appearance. These are not the events of life enjoyed by ambitious young dreamers.

One day his dad, Jesse, decided that David needed to mix it up a little, and so he sent him on special assignment. He was to deliver some bread and cheese to his three older brothers and their unit who were on the frontlines against the enemy Philistines. Ever eager to get in on the action, David readily made his way to the encampment, dropped off the supplies, and headed straight for the battlefield.

There he was chatting with his brothers when suddenly emerging from the Philistine's line was a gargantuan human doing. His name was Goliath, a name that has become synonymous with the monsters, giants, and challenges of every generation since the story was first told. We don't know exactly everything he was saying, but we can speculate that Goliath was probably spouting off at the mouth about how spineless the Israelites were, and how if their God looked anything like them, then he was certain they would be slaves by sundown. You know. The stuff you say when you are trying to pick a fight. He was also proposing a challenge to make this whole Israeli and Philistine showdown a little simpler. All the Israelites needed to do was pick one dude. Whomever they thought was their best warrior. Send him down to face Goliath in a no holds barred ultimate fighting match. Whomever walked away the winner was the winner for their whole country. The losing team would surrender to the other side. A multitude of soldiers would not have to die, the battle could be over relatively quickly as opposed to the typical all day battle, and the decision as to who the winner was would be clear cut. Like all good human doings, Goliath had a plan. He had the whole thing figured out. What David seemed to find the most appalling about this moment was not the stench of this giant or even the horrendous accusations he was making about his God, faith, or people. What he could not understand is why somebody had not already stepped up to the plate and closed the mouth of this numbskull once and for all. It seemed that all of these great Israelite warriors, including his own brothers, that he had looked up to, that he had come to watch the heroics of on the battlefield, were all defining FEAR the wrong way. No one was wanting to step into the middle of this valley turned coliseum. No one was volunteering to actually face the giant. The prevailing definition of FEAR here seemed to be Forget Everything And Run.

David's time of shepherding had afforded him a lot of what most of us would consider to be a boring time of just being. As mind numbing as such a job might seem to our modern sensibilities, it had provided David much time for contemplation and practice. Time to think about who he was created to be, what he was and was not good at, the things he was afraid of, and the occasional opportunity that would come along to test his merit against such fears. Two separate incidences had involved at one time a bear and the other a lion. On both occasions all of David's slingshot practice during his down time came in very handy. He had been able to successfully neutralize the predators before any harm had come to his flock. Now looking down into this valley all David could see was the ultimate predator. One that was not just placing his sheep in jeopardy, but was threatening the very existence of his people. Maybe even more daunting than the predator that was bellowing in front of him was the realization that everyone around him had come to misdefine FEAR, and the resulting aftermath would be their demise if he did not step up in this moment and show them the proper definition.

After some haggling with Saul, the king of the Israelites, and some big time pushback from his brothers, David finally convinced everyone that the right approach was to take this giant head on, believing that God would take care of the rest. It was time to teach his soon to be people–in case I hadn't mentioned it yet, David would ultimately become the king of the Israelites–the proper definition of FEAR. Face Everything And Recover.

David was not going to be using the latest battle gear for this encounter. It had been offered to him, but he readily admitted that he didn't really know how to use such weaponry, and that it wasn't really in keeping with his simplistic style. What this moment called for was what had become a tried and true method for David. His God, a slingshot, and his willingness to face the monster versus running from it.

Lots of practice had taught David exactly what kind of stones to choose for his slingshot. Picking the right stones would help to determine how easily the rock was released from the pouch, the speed at which it traveled, and most importantly the trajectory. Eliminating all unnecessary impediments was going to be key to a quick victory. He bent down by the stream and carefully chose his ammunition–five smooth stones. Rumor was that Goliath had a few brothers, and so having a few more rocks in his arsenal was a good insurance policy. He then proceeded to become a timeless example of how to properly define the ever so present reality that every human doing experiences–FEAR. David demonstrated how defining FEAR as Face Everything And Recover versus Forget Everything And Run was the first step in the transformation from human doing into becoming human. David walked into the valley and he faced his giant!

So I am believing that earlier in this chapter you took the time to go on a journey of self discovery and named your fear or fears, as well as unveiled some of their points of origin in your life's story. That was work well done. The next step is to pick up the first stone. Decide on the first step of action you are going to take to overcome what has been holding you back. It may be a letter that needs to be written to someone who has hurt you. It could be sitting down with your boss and having that crucial conversation. It is possibly calling Weight Watchers or walking into your first Alcoholics Anonymous meeting. Whatever it may be, decide on one simple thing you can do to begin advancing, ask a friend to encourage you in your step, and get to walking toward your fear instead of running away from it. You don't have to know the outcome. David didn't. All you have to do is quit running. All you have to do is pick up that first stone and make that first step toward facing your fear.

Oh, and do you want to know the outcome of the story with David? Well, I was nice enough to tell you where you could go and find it, but just as a reminder it is in that crazy Old Testament book of the Bible, 1 Samuel chapter 17.

One thing you will not find in 1 Samuel 17 is an answer as to how I gashed my ear. Well here we go. Drumroll please! The best I can tell is that I had actually passed out with the top of an open beer can pressed against my ear for an extended period of time as I slept. Yes folks, this is how goofy and tragic life can get when we run. You can slice your ear on a beer can while sleeping. One more example of how all those weird warning labels get attached to products, and you wonder why they would have to warn someone not to do something so stupid in the first place.

The worst part of it all is that on that day I did not quit running. I got my ear patched up, went to work and told my colleagues that I had run into a door in the dark; I vowed to never return to the doctor again under my own cognitive will, and climbed in bed with a beer again that evening. Running was my modus operandi. It's the only thing my human doing knew how to do when faced with my deepest fears. I had many more miles to run before the wake up call. Thank God it finally came.

Save yourself a trip to the Patient First clinic, and the most embarrassing chapter of a book. Decide to approach life as a human being. Define FEAR the right way. Name what it is that you are so scared of—and it may not be just one thing. You may have a list. That's okay. The monster loses all of its "boo" power when it no longer has a closet to hide in or a dark room in which to cloak itself. Sit until you discover what your fear is. Name it. Pick up your first stone, and determine to Face Everything And Recover. You got this!

It's Not All About Me

One of the things you have to learn fast if you are going to recover from addiction is to just tell the truth already! After years of lying to yourself and everybody around you, otherwise known as denial, it just comes time to come clean. That is the first step to getting clean. There will be more about that to come later in these musings, but for now just highlight it and know that's why I am about to make the following confession.

I am a totally, completely, absolutely, unquestionably, doubtlessly (you get the point because of so many adverbs) self-absorbed human doing. I wrote that right, human doing. Case in point, I started that last sentence with "I", and my sophomore English teacher taught me I should never do that. Who cares! I already passed that class, and this is about me, isn't it?

A good thing about throwing down this egocentric truth right off the bat is that now this book will sell more than just a copy to my mom. I'll have friends and family lining up for the book signing asking me to put my Hancock on the last paragraph, and reminding me that I said it, they didn't. My sister will probably buy enough copies to make it a New York Times bestseller.

But, it's true. I am selfish and that results in my human doingness. That results in my need to own, control, and get credit for nearly everything—well, everything good of course. Someone else can take the blame for the bad stuff. Those needs lead to focusing on stuff not spirit, progress not people, and fame not what's for real. That focus leads to feelings of fear, resentment, and a whole lot of stress.

***

It was a Wednesday morning, and this was supposed to be the first day of the rest of my life. But, it had started out just like every other day of my life had started for some time: with beer. It was the only way to get my system rolling in the morning without the extreme nausea of withdrawal from the night before. Not much of an existence, I realize, but it was what I had come to know of life. Each sip of this morning's beer felt special, carrying with it a sentimental value that only a true connoisseur—read addict—can understand. In theory, each sip was one syllable in a long goodbye to an old, untrustworthy yet cherished friend. Alcohol. On this day, I was going to rehab.

Yeah, I was getting drunk the morning I was headed to rehab. Living out my human doing right up until the end by doing the thing I had learned to do best. While I thought I was being clever with this final salvo, it would turn out that this is nothing more than classic addiction behavior. Most of my fellow rehabies would arrive under some form of intoxication. It was all about what I wanted right up until the end.

In spite of all this selfishness there were many people who had already surrounded me with undeserved love and support. More than one had offered to drive me the hour and a half up the road to where I would be spending the next twenty eight days of my life. While I was thankful for each declaration of solidarity on this impending journey, I knew that there was only one who was up for the task. It was my best friend, Tally.

***

Now before we get too far into thinking this book is about recovering from chemical addiction, let's recognize it's not. It's about the fact that we were all born into this world with some amazing promise. Created in the image of God. Created as a human being. Stop and let that sink in for just a second. This means that when you look in the mirror, the image staring back at you represents at the very subatomic and soul level the particles of God's creative breath energizing your physical and spiritual existence. You are no small achievement. You are one of the greatest pronouncements of God's imagination in the history of the universe. Boom! Take that to your next annual review and see if it doesn't get you a bump up the pay scale.

The problem we create with having all this awesomeness wired into our genetic code is that we too early in life come to believe we are the only one that has it, or at least that we have more than everybody else around us. We forget, ignore, or outright deny that this awesomeness has a Source beyond ourselves, and that this awesomeness was designed to show off the awesomeness of its Source as well as connect with all the awesomeness in others. This awesomeness doesn't have to prove itself by doing anything. It's awesome. It was created that way by the one who is Awesome. Stay connected to that realization and all is good. Try to prove it through human doing and that is where things start to go south. All we have to do is be. Instead, we opt to declare our awesomeness as absolute and come to see the beautiful world around us as nothing more than a place full of people to serve our awesome's interest. This is why when we start doing things: nations invade, races enslave, corporations pollute, religions condemn, gangs kill, spouses abuse, families manipulate, and kids push. My awesome is more awesome than your awesome. Let me prove it! It's the reason we all get addicted to something. We have to comfort our awesomeness when we are faced with the reality that awesomeness is not ours alone. It's been given to us by Another.

This book is about recovering the original intent of our God-given awesomeness. Rediscovering our place as human beings, and not being driven by an obsession to prove ourselves to ourselves, others, or God. Recovering from the fact that the world is not all about us. Rediscover our created image. Having a best friend to drive you to rehab is as good a place to begin as any. A real friend reminds you that you are awesome just being the original you. That there is awesome outside of you to which you can connect, and that any awesome you feel has forever been lost is really not gone, just temporarily incapacitated, or in my case, inebriated.

***

By God's grace, I had just finished the last alcoholic beverage I will ever consume by choice when Tally pulled up. I lugged the suitcase into the back of his trunk and we were off to destination incarceration. That is what it feels like when you are headed to rehab, unless you are really strange and somewhere along the way you have placed "rehab" on your bucket list. That is what I tried telling people in rehab when I first got there. That I was there because it was on my bucket list. No one was buying the line.

Tally was exactly who God had orchestrated for this moment. He didn't try to condemn me for the one last party I had thrown myself that morning and the alcohol I am sure he could smell on my breath. He didn't try to give me any advice, because he knew others would be offering plenty of that in the days to come. He did encourage me by saying, "John, this experience is going to be great for you! Where else could you go where you get to talk about yourself and be the center of attention for twenty-eight days?" From a guy with an ego as big as mine, when he put it that way, it didn't sound so bad. From there we told old stories, laughed till we cried, and did something I was rarely doing in those days, dream of our futures. He simply did what real friends do. He saw me in my need and rather than merely offering "help," he simply walked with me as far as he could in the journey.

It takes many people playing various roles for us to recover from our human doing in order to become a human being again. In my case that included my ever-loving wife and kids, mom, dad, sister, in-laws, my pastor and fellow church staff members, our congregation, many friends spread across the country, and no less than five—yes, I said five—professional counselors. But, only one person could walk me all the way up to the doors of rehab. My best friend. Thanks Tally!

Here's where it gets interesting though. They don't let your friends join you in rehab. Probably for good reason. You have to walk in alone.

***

When you have lost your human being and made all your doing about yourself, being alone is something that you get used to experiencing. The reason is you are disconnected from your awesomeness Source and the awesomeness of others. I've sat in a room on many occasions listening to a conversation and even engaging the topic only to feel like the Scrooge observing Tiny Tim and family through the window on Christmas Day with no one even knowing he was there. You have a secret to keep. You are not as awesome as you have made yourself out to be. All your doing has covered up your being. No one can know the real truth. That means you are alone.

Walking through the doors of rehab was much more than being alone. Don't get me wrong. There was a nice young lady with a big smile offering to tell me what was next, but I couldn't remember what she said if I had to, because everything happening around me was completely consumed by what felt like a black hole of loneliness. It was not as if I was just observing and nobody knew I was there, it was more like I no longer existed. I haven't figured it all out yet, but I'm pretty sure this is part of what Jesus meant when He said that thing about if you want to keep your life you have to lose it. Until we get to the point where we feel that our own awesomeness has ceased to exist and cannot exist apart from its original Source, then real healing won't begin. Until we understand that everything we do does not create who we are, then we won't really begin to live.

It didn't take me very long to pass through the black hole and realize that I did in fact exist and that this was happening. My first sign of life was the unbelievable embarrassment I felt as over the course of the next few hours I got to breathe into a breathalyzer, be poked and prodded, and even ushered into a room where I put on a cute little hospital gown–I look great in blue–to make it easier for the search ensuring I had not smuggled any contraband. I assure you that if Sandy Berger had hid classified papers where they searched me–instead of his socks–he would have never been caught. The best part was when they asked, "Profession?"

"Uhhh? Pastor?"

Minutes felt like hours, but by early afternoon they looked at me and said, "Have a great day! You're free until supper." What? This wasn't exactly like being dropped off at Disney World. I thought these people knew what they were doing. I thought the healing was supposed to begin. Immediately! Didn't they know that you can't leave an alcoholic unattended? There was nothing to do! Worst of all the morning's buzz was gone, and believe it or not there was no bar available with Happy Hour specials. How inconsiderate. This place stunk bad.

There was no way I could sit still, because my anxiety level was too high. This was a combination of withdrawal and having to be here in the first place. Thankfully, it was a beautiful campus, so I decided to take a hike. Earlier in the day while taking the tour all the different buildings had been pointed out to me, but I wasn't paying much attention. This was the chance to acclimate myself with the place, and actually make note of how to get around. A few minutes into my walk I saw a building that struck me with an air of familiarity. I am sure it was the shape, as well as the presence of a few stained glass windows that caught my attention. Welcome to the chapel.

Now I don't believe that an infinite, eternal God can in any way be housed inside of a building built less than fifty years ago, nor that by throwing a few religious symbols on the walls He somehow likes to hang out there more than in the beauty of the great cathedral of the outdoors that He designed. Can you imagine God saying, "Wow! I'm really glad you built this place for me. It's always too hot or too cold out there. As long as you keep it at 71 degrees, I'll never want to leave." No, we build these buildings for our own religious and cultural convenience, but on this particular day I could sense that He was calling me to an appointment inside, and did I ever have a reason why I wanted to meet with Him. God had some explaining to do.

***

There is this guy named Dean that has had a significant impact on my life. Mind you I have never met him, and never will on this side of eternity. I feel like I know him pretty well though, and if there was some way to run into one another while occupying different dimensions of existence, we would probably be able to talk as friends who have been acquainted for awhile. At a minimum of at least five days a week I get to sit in the space where his creative energies use to construct amazing experiences for people to connect with God. When I leave what I guess could be considered "our" office and walk down the hall to see my administrative assistant, Gwen, I can see him standing there on stage in a Hawaiian shirt with microphone in hand living the experience he had imagined. It's one of Gwen's most prized pictures; Dean leading our church in a worship service.

Several years ago Dean was diagnosed with pancreatic cancer. If you have ever known someone who has received this unfortunate diagnosis, then you are aware that far too often it carries with it a rather heavy sentence. If there was ever a person for whom to ponder the question of why bad things happen to good people, then everyone who knew and loved Dean would have told you he, and they, had the right to ask.

My pastor, Drew, was not just Dean's boss and colleague, but also one of his closest friends. Drew made the decision early on that no matter what this meant, Dean would have somebody by his side the whole time, and even if he walked through the valley of the shadow of death he would not do it alone. As you are starting to see, it's just the type of guy my pastor is.

For two years they would spend a lot of time together in hospitals and medical facilities for chemo and surgery. Although they were both men of faith they wrestled deeply with that question. Why do bad things happen to good people? One wondering why this was happening to a friend, and the other asking why this was happening to himself. This type of thing just doesn't seem fair. It also doesn't always have an answer.

My pastor tears up a bit just about every time he tells the story. On one of his final times in the hospital with Dean— before he would journey into the eternal—Dean had a Spirit induced epiphany concerning that ever pressing question. Dean looked at Drew and said, "What if this isn't about me?"

Although I had heard this story on many occasions and marveled at the faith of Dean in coming to accept such difficult circumstances with such selflessness, I had never thought that this was a great foretelling of things to come in my own life and story. I had yet to see the lesson that was there for me in being able to ask the question, "What if this isn't about me?" That was all about to change.

I walked through the doors of the chapel thankful to find that there was no one else there. God had arranged this to be a private meeting. Good thing for Him. I had some things I needed to say, and it would be better for Him if He didn't have to try and defend Himself in front of an audience. I decided to forgo all the normal formalities like, "Dear Heavenly Father," because that was the last thing for which I was going to be giving Him credit. I dove straight in with, "How dare You, You *&%#, *&^%, #$%^, %^&*, and *&^%!" My mother would not have been proud of me for using such language, especially at God, and frankly I am even a little scared that she will be reading this. (Hey Mom, haven't I given you the most amazing grandkids? Smile!)

***

You will recall David, who we met in the last chapter; the boy who kicked Goliath's butt. That is really putting it nicely considering what he actually did to him. David grew up to be one of the early kings of Israel, back a few thousand years ago when they were a monarchy. Not everyone is aware that David was also quite the songwriter. While he didn't leave any of his sheet music behind, most of his lyrics are still with us, and musicians are still creating melodies to bring his words to song.

These Psalms, as they are known, can be found smack dab in the middle of just about any Bible that you pick up. If you ever get the chance to read any of them you will discover they cover some pretty heavy subject matter. Often David starts out questioning God on why He allows the things He does. Sometimes he downright accuses God of seeming injustices committed against both himself and others. A few times he gets contrite about his own actions, like the time he slept with a dude's wife, and then had him killed so that it wouldn't be found out, and he is basically begging God not to smash Him into a greasy spot. Nonetheless, David is real with God.

This is all that I was doing. Getting real with God. Sure, I chose a few words that David didn't have at his disposal, but then again after his little tryst with Bathsheba progressing to murder of her husband Uriah, he probably wasn't wanting to draw further attention to himself with an "explicit lyrics" label attached to his album. I'm not advocating coming at God the way I did. Just telling my story. I would say you're not going to get anywhere until you start the conversation though, so do what you've got to do.

After my temper subsided a bit, I started to lay out the case against God as I saw it. I wanted to know why the heck I was in rehab. I wanted to know why I was an alcoholic. Why had this happened to me, and how did I get here? Wasn't He aware of my awesomeness?

I had been born into a great family. I had many great opportunities in life. I started serving people long before anyone else my age. I chose a profession that was all about doing stuff for Him. I had never experienced any real tragedies or abuse. I dealt with people that had extreme predilections and addictions all the time. I could see with their backgrounds how they had become dependent. I had no excuse! Why would He let this happen to me? Sure, I started drinking with friends in high school, but plenty of them had not turned out as alcoholics. Why me? If this case seems to be a jumbled mess, it's because it was.

Have you noticed how many sentences in the last paragraph started with "I"? "I" and what "I" had done seemed to be the only common theme I brought in my case.

Here is what happened next. Nothing. I had just ranted and raved for well over an hour, calling God everything I could think of, and blaming Him in every way I could. What do I get in return? Nothing. He didn't even smash me into a greasy spot. Total silence. That was Wednesday.

Thursday and Friday were spent getting used to the routine that would be my life for the next month. Up at 6 AM. Nurses station. Get dressed. Breakfast. Lecture. Group therapy. Lunch. Nurses Station. Classes. Lecture. More Lecture. Structured Leisure. Dinner. Lecture. A.A. Meeting. Nurses Station. Snack with friends. Read. Lights out. Sleep. Up at 6 AM. Ad nauseam repeat. What did I hear from God? Nothing.

Saturday. Would you believe people who work at a rehab facility like to go home and be with their families on the weekend? As a result, the place was pretty dead. Lots of free time on my hands. Could have another discussion with God? No thanks. If He's not talking, then I wasn't about to either.

Sunday.

Sunday, has always been a pretty significant day in my life. Not only am I a pastor, but I grew up as pastor's kid, so if nothing else, it has always been the busiest. The tie to Sunday being a busy day for a pastor goes back a long way, and anyone who has ever attended a church Easter service has probably picked up a clue as to what the connection is. It all has to do with this God-man named Jesus who was brutally murdered by the religious and political authorities of his day, and then just when the murderers thought they had done the right thing and put the agitator of their awesomeness to rest, His grave shows up empty on a Sunday. He starts making appearances all around the region declaring that He is not dead. His teachings live too, and there is hope for all of humanity, or at least for anyone who is willing to pay attention and love out His message. In short, personal, political, and religious awesomeness and doing mean nothing if they are not attached to their Source, and Jesus is their Source. Thus, Sunday has become a pretty big deal for life changing messages. On this Sunday, I would hear mine.

This is one of those times when I wished I had a novelist eye and could crank out a synomic avalanche of brilliant adjectives to describe what the morning sun looked like hovering over the Chesapeake Bay, but since that's not going to happen, suffice it to say it looked amazing. As I walked over and took a seat on a wooden chair overlooking the bay to enjoy the view before heading to the morning chapel experience, I was comparing what I had learned about addiction over the first few days of rehab with my own family's background and history.

Turns out that over the course of the last few years of my active addiction, I had begun to uncover the faintest of hints that addiction, as well as mental health challenges, had bore fruit in my own family tree. As a result of having skipped a generation I had never been directly aware, but the indirect reality that the innate brokenness of my family had found its way into my genetic space was now all too real. I mean, I was in rehab. The cycle of addiction, if not properly accounted for and subsequently broken, breeds the cycle of addiction. Doing will breed more doing.

The crazy part about chemical addiction is you never know if your body and brain are hardwired for it until you actually ingest the chemical. With addiction being part of my family tree it meant that my chances of winning the alcoholic jackpot was that much higher. Little did I know that when I took my first drink around seventeen years old, I was playing a game of Russian roulette with multiple bullets in the chambers. I am not shirking responsibility for any action I have taken while under the influence, or in the pursuit of my drug of choice. For every way in which I have hurt or harmed another human being, or myself as a result of my alcoholism, I am fully responsible. However, to religiously simplify issues such as alcoholism or other "sins" as to their right or wrongness, and not account for their broader connotations, can result in misunderstanding the real nature of that person's wound, as well as devalue opportunities for their healing and subsequent reversal of ill effects on future generations. When I was growing up, my family had never known this stuff. They didn't know addiction was a physical family thing. It was simply seen as the temporary shortcoming of a few in the family line, never to be spoken about for sake of those individuals' reputations. They could only warn me of the generalized potential and moral peril of taking my first drink, not the personal likelihood that I would be switching on a gene I could never switch off by myself. This is the litany of thought that was running through my head as I sat on that bench. Then I heard the question resurface. The question that I had never considered could be more than a final revelation of a guy I had never met named Dean. The question that I had never considered might be applicable for me and my own life's trial and trauma.

"Maybe, it's not about you?"

After silence for more than three days it would seem that God had decided I had simmered down just enough to potentially hear His response. After my tirade and His subsequent quiet, I figured it would be best if I listened for once.

"Maybe, it's not about you. Don't get me wrong, you blew it. It's one of the reasons you are in this place. It's a nice place by the way, maybe you should be thanking Me for that. Like the view?

You're here because you got a distorted idea about the awesomeness I gave you. You're here because you've been doing a whole lot to prove your awesomeness versus just being who I made you to be. You're here because we need to get to the bottom of some things and find out what's really irking you. You're here because I love you, and rather than turn you into a greasy spot—you seem to think I like turning people into greasy spots—I'll free you from your own delusion and give you a second chance. And finally, you being here may not be all about you!

You remember that young guy that came to talk to you through your own tear stained eyes last Sunday, a few minutes after the whole church found out you were an alcoholic? The one that told you of his own concern that he had a problem with addiction? Maybe, I've used your public misadventure to lead him to his own personal recovery?

Or how about those three amazing kids I gave you? You heard the other day in an addiction education class how they have an 80% chance of becoming an addict should they ever try a substance. Maybe, I am using this moment to prune addiction out of your family tree? At the very least I'm giving them a little more ammo against their own potential brokenness to come.

I'll have a lot more to say to you over the course of the next few weeks while I have you in here, but get one thing straight. This is not all about you." - God a.k.a. Your Heavenly Father

Please don't think these were the exact words God used. It was the general point of what I heard and felt in that moment of being reunited with His voice. It is the point I attempt to remind myself on a daily basis, so that I can stay properly connected to my Source of awesomeness and the awesomeness in others. So that I can just be human.

I'm not sure what you call your version of rehab, or storm that you just faced, are facing, or will face in the near future. I don't know if it has come or will come in the form of a self-inflicted wound like mine, selfish and abusive behavior of another, undeserved diagnosis of a disease, or tragic separation from one you love. No matter. One thing I learned from the courageous example of Dean and my own experience in rehab is that it's worth considering, "Maybe, it's not all about you?"

Forget Everything You Know

As a kid I remember sitting on the couch one day looking around at all the stuff that was in our house. There were pictures on the wall, a room full of furniture, knick knacks of no sentimental value, but properly placed to occupy open space. Americans can never let it appear that we can't afford to have something sitting in every nook and cranny. That could ruin the Feng Shui of both the room and our reputations. And as I thought about it, this was just one room. Every room in the house was like this, and for all over exaggerated purposes we were poor! My question sitting there was, "How does one get all this stuff? It would cost a fortune to buy all of this. No way would I ever be able to have all this when I grew up." Boy, was I wrong.

Fast forward to present day life having achieved a good career, seventeen years of marriage, and three Crazies—that's the loving moniker I have given my kids. It was time for the garage to get cleaned out!

We had only been living in our house for five years, but we had been avoiding this project for the full seventeen years of our marriage. We had made a few feeble attempts in the past, but if we were going to take steps toward the hip new minimalist trend sweeping the nation, or at least that's what the documentaries make it look like, then we had some major destuffinization to do.

As Saturday morning dawned, the garage door rose, and the decluttering began. Now you know how this works. Step number one is just to get everything outside the garage and spread it all over the driveway, lawn, and neighbors lawn so you could actually see what you have. Step number two is make a sign that says, "This is not a garage sale. Keep driving!" We did not take this step which resulted in multiple interruptions, and angry folks who were looking to find an authentic Picasso that mistakenly found its way into a suburban household that they could buy on the cheap, have it's value appraised on the Antique Roadshow, sell it at auction, and go retire in the Florida Keys. Step number three is the one that is long and laborious. It is also the one that can cause the most emotional distress, start civil wars, and ensure that the family therapist has enough hours logged to provide an amazing Christmas for her kids. I'm talking about sorting.

Now the key to good sorting is to establish ground rules that everybody can agree to right up front. They will not do you any good as soon as your little girl cries because that is her "favorite stuffie" that she hasn't seen in five years, and to put it in the giveaway pile would mean the end of her childhood as she knows it, but ground rules will at least help you feel as if you had a semblance of control over this operation for at least a good two minutes. The second thing you have to do is determine what each pile is to be labeled. For our project we kept it simple with a pile for trash, a pile for donation, a pile to keep, and a pile for we don't quite know yet, but will figure it out at the end.

The interesting thing about this type of project is how gung-ho it starts out, with a real belief that by mid afternoon you'll be a newly inaugurated minimalist. Such ambition at first causes you to grab and chunk everything in sight, until you catch yourself doing a double take at the giveaway pile, and reconsidering the sentimental value of that souvenir coffee cup from Sea World that you got when you were eight and Flipper was still a household name. Each object begins to be treated with greater scrutiny so as not to make such a near wasteful choice twice. As if the debate over each item that now ensues in your own head and subsequently moves to a debate with your spouse is not enough to slow this already tedious process down, after a few hours you start to reach the bottom of the garage. This is where all the stuff lies that has survived previous attempts at turning the garage into a man cave. It was here that I found it.

For some reason that I cannot possibly comprehend, I had a huge box full of old college notes and graded papers. They had probably been kept because my ego is so self aggrandizing that I thought they would someday be used as examples of young genius when my biographies were written. (The dynamic opinions of a human doing. Anything to help out the future historians!) The best thing to do on this type of find when cleaning a garage is to just chunk it without peaking. To open Pandora's box by taking a look at what's really there is to start the whole mental rollercoaster of should it stay, or should it go? So what do you think I did?

Of course, I opened it and looked!

What I found there was appalling, because the truth is I had always prided myself on being a pretty good student. As I began to shuffle through the papers I was taken aback on many fronts. Papers that had been marked as A's or B's would begin with a sentence making a broad and often undocumented claim. How did the professor not just throw it away at that moment? What I found worse were the arguments themselves. How could I have ever believed that, or argued for such a position? So much in my little mind had changed since the unexperienced days when these ideas were written.

Although I found this to be a bit depressing, I tried not to let it influence my view of my alma mater, since I consider it to be such a stellar institution from which the greatest minds of this generation graduate. Oops, there's that ego again. Sorry.

I had dared to peak and now the mental minimalist war was raging within my head. Should it stay, or should it go? Wouldn't my children someday want to read, "Dad: The Early Years"? Wouldn't this be a good reminder in future reads as to how far I had intellectually progressed? What about the historians? So much insight for the ages could be lost! These writings were a memorial to the power of human doing. Then I remembered something I had learned early on in my rehab experience.

Forget everything you know.

I'll let you in on a little secret of the recovery community, since that's one of the side benefits of this book anyhow. We recovering addicts love to use short, pithy, one liners that are really easy to remember. Phrases you have probably heard like, "One day at a time." or "Your struggle is part of your story." One of my counselors explained that it is because we have so altered our mental capacities, or in other words fried our brains, that it's the easiest way to grasp the necessary concepts in early recovery. I haven't questioned this theory. It sounds pretty logical to me.

It was early on in rehab that I was introduced to the concept of "forget everything you know." I hated it! As I have mentioned multiple times already, I am really smart. Did I mention that I am really smart? At least this is the line that I have fed myself most of my life, but not in the "say it and believe it" type of way. It has been more say it, because I didn't believe it, so I would say it some more. My human doing demanded it.

This never-ending cycle of unbelief in my intellectual capacity, followed by the false faith reinforcement of my intellectual prowess by my ego, had led me to a never-ending cycle of self doubt that I supplemented by telling myself I was fine and was human doing it all right. I guess that could be considered a long definition of denial. Forget everything you know is not what you want to hear when you are in denial, because everything you know is what you are relying on to maintain what you have defined as your sanity.

If everything you know is taken away, then what is there? I had built my whole life on what I know. My family looked to me for what I know. As a pastor, people show up every week to hear what I know. I was paid well for what I know. I am good at Jeopardy. You want me to forget everything I know? Crazy!

Then one of the rehab speakers had the audacity to say it like this, "Your best thinking got you here." Ouch!

Take a moment to think about where you are right now. I'm not talking about the coffee shop, bookstore aisle, or airport where you are reading this, I'm talking about where you are in life. You may find yourself at the rock bottom of an addiction, and that's why you picked up this book. Or, you may be at the pinnacle of success, and just wanted to pick up the latest New York Times bestseller. (You think if I mention the New York Times bestseller list enough times that they'll put me on it?) Anyhow, wherever you are in life it is the result of your very best thinking up until now. Every step you have taken has led you to your current destination, and each step had a guiding thought that spurred it forward. Every business you own and every credit card bill you have, every muscle you show off or roll of fat you hide, every "I love you" you have uttered, or the first time you screamed "divorce" in an argument with your spouse, all are the result of a seed of thought that was planted in that mental muscle between your ears called a brain. That seed sprouted, and here you are. Your best thinking got you here.

Now I know the natural human tendency is to argue, well what about circumstances that are out of my control? I didn't choose cancer, a market crash, or life altering injury. And you would be right in saying that, but it's dangerous when we believe those things alone have brought us to a state of lacking fulfillment, when in reality it is a series of thoughts or stories we have built around those unwanted circumstances that have led us to our current destination. A chapter on that later. For now, let's stick with *your best thinking got you here*. Your best thinking caused you to do what you have done as a human doing.

I was not finding this new reality to be very encouraging. I was in rehab. All my smartness, and this is where it had led me. Rehab certainly signaled that it was time for change, and the lesson seemed to be that it was my thinking that needed to change most. I was going to have to forget everything I knew. I was going to have to open my mind to some new possibilities. I was going to have to listen to what someone else thought and had to say. I needed to be in the congregation taking notes rather than doing the preaching.

***

My situation reminded me of this unfamiliar story tucked away in the Old Testament of the Bible in the book of 2 Kings chapter 5. There is this guy named Naaman. Turns out he is the commander of the army of this really powerful King of Aram. Naaman being a powerful general is not what reminded me of my situation, in case you think my ego is running away with me again. What we had in common was disease.

Now if I had to pick between the disease he had or alcoholism, then I would definitely go with alcoholism. Both can and will kill you, but his would eventually cause a zombie like persona leading to his face falling off. Sorry, for that visual. He had leprosy. He is a super smart and powerful leader whose ultimate fate would likely be banishment to a colony of lepers and then a horrifying and agonizing death where his skin slowly disintegrated off of his body. I can think of better ways to go. There was no natural cure for leprosy. Under normal circumstances Naaman was doomed.

It so happened that during one of Naaman's many conquest he had captured a little Israelite girl and had brought her back to his wife to work as her maid. This servant girl couldn't help but notice that Naaman wasn't looking so hot. Leprosy is one of those illnesses that's kind of hard to hide. One day she mentioned to the lady of the house that there was this guy back in her homeland of Samaria who she thought Naaman might ought to go see. She knew some good things about this prophet of God named Elisha, and thought he might be able to help out. She was a lot kinder than I am. Not sure I would have been throwing get well tips at my captor, but she was still young enough to recognize that the healing power of God should be available to everyone, even if they are your enemy.

Naaman ran it by his king, got a leave of absence from work, and was off to see Elisha. So far, so good.

Most of us can at least get this far. We know that something in life has got to give. Something has to change. We don't think we can bear the pain of our circumstances any longer. The weight has to go, the job has to change, the relationship has to evolve, or else we are going to lose our minds. Whatever we are doing is not working. We start to make positive moves when the pain gets intense enough. We begin to watch documentaries to compare the best diets. We research what type of training might be available for a career change, and we read a few books on how to win friends and get that special person to love us again for the first time. This is akin to opening the garage and declaring today is the day for a clean up, and finding the system for accomplishing it.

***

A year prior to my rehab experience I had come to the point that the pain was unbearable and I had to open the garage door of my life. It was summer, and whereas some folks get to slow down and take it a little easier, that is not the case for the role that I play in my professional church life. During the summer my pastor will often take a much deserved extended vacation, which means that for that period of time I often wear two hats including speaking in his stead for our weekend services. This particular summer's responsibilities had even been heavier with a few outside speaking opportunities including a beach camp for middle schoolers in South Carolina. This would mean that in just one particular week I would speak a total of nineteen times. Now I realize that there are supermen of communication that exist and publicly speak way more often, but for a guy who was hiding an addiction to alcohol it was a bit much. It was a lot of hiding and trying to find creative ways to weave the addiction into a jam packed "God glorifying" schedule. Probably goes without saying that the tension was building and becoming unmanageable.

Driving home from the office on a Wednesday afternoon I actually had a moment where I thought I was going crazy. If something else didn't break, then I would. The end felt as if it were near. How it would come, either negatively or positively, I didn't care. I just knew the pain, fear, and loneliness had to end. For the next few days I existed soberly only when I had to.

On Sunday afternoon, I had just settled in for some rest after a long morning of faking it with the church, when I received a text with a link to an article from my best friend, Tally, whom I have already introduced to you. It was an unassuming article about what was happening in the world of "church news" that day. Unfortunately, it was an article of yet another well known pastor blessed with having had immense impact who was having to step down from his position, and in this case it was because of his relationship with alcohol. For purposes I will explain later, I share that it was Perry Noble. My heart dropped twelve inches into my guttural region. I've seen a lot of pastors stumble forward for a lot of reasons, but this guy was plagued by the same demons as me. Immediately, I realized that all my fears could and would come true. If he could be impacted to the point that he was having to step away from his ministry, then certainly a no name like myself could slip into the dimension of ministerial nothingness with no one ever having noticed. No one would ever know what my human doing had done. At the time this potential loss to my ego seemed unbearable. Like Naaman, something had to change.

***

Naaman, along with his entourage, made the journey and arrived to see the famed prophet. Now when you're a guy like Naaman you are use to a little fanfare when you arrive. If someone doesn't show you the proper type of respect, then that is why you have an entourage of special forces. They can encourage folks to step up their hospitality game on your behalf. When Naaman arrived Elisha did not even bother coming to the door.

There's a quick side lesson on this one. The people that can help you out the most in life don't really care about your title or accomplishments. They are more concerned with who you are and who you can be, not what you are and what you do or have done.

Elisha sent his messenger to the door and delivered some fairly straightforward instructions, "Go and wash yourself seven times in the Jordan River. Then your skin will be restored, and you will be healed of your leprosy."

Naaman was livid!

***

I picked up the phone and called Tally. I don't remember the exact words of the conversation, but I certainly remember the sentiment on both sides. I confessed to him that I was an alcoholic, and that it was time to get some help. Curiously, I inquired as to whether or not he knew what he was doing when he sent me that article. He said he was not aware that I was an alcoholic, but he had begun to wonder as a result of a few observations if there wasn't a growing problem. He offered me the greatest words of comfort in those moments. Reminding me of the grace of God that I had been blessed to introduce to so many in ministry life over the years, and now it was my turn to fall back into His arms of grace and let Him take it from there. I would see that grace through my friend who would be there for me through every step of this journey.

Over the course of the next few days I went to see an awesome Jesus-centered counselor for the first time, and told him what was going on, and that no one knew but my wife and best friend. This began periods of abstinence from alcohol for me as I began attending meetings, and dipping my toes in the waters of recovery.

My counselor continued to encourage me to find someone in one of my support meetings who had enjoyed sobriety for some time, and connect with them in a way where they could give me advice and encouragement that could only come from their own success in this journey of recovery. I hem-hawed around for as long as I could, coming up with a variety of excuses and obstacles as to why finding someone like this was so much harder than it looked. The pressure was growing, and I finally walked up to a guy at one of the meetings. I asked him what the possibilities of connecting for some advice might look like. He asked me a little bit about my story, gave me his number and said to call him the next day at 4:00PM.

I left the meeting ecstatic! I had found my guy. I could get my counselor off my back. And, I could prove to my boss—as I knew I would have to soon—that while I had this problem, I was doing the right things to "fix it."

Problem was, 4:00PM came and went the next day, and I made no phone call. No phone call meant not going back to the meetings, because there's no way you can see the guy that said to call when you didn't call. No meetings meant lying to the counselor, and being back in the shadows of deception meant it would not be long before I was drinking again. Little did I know at the time this was classic alcoholic behavior. Really, classic human doing behavior. I had done all the research and chosen a plan of action. I just wasn't ready to forget everything that had led me to this place quite yet.

***

Naaman could't believe that he had been snubbed by this so called prophet of God. He couldn't believe that he had traveled all that way and used all those resources to simply be told to go and dip in the dirty waters of the Jordan river. If Elisha was all that, then couldn't he just wave his hand and invoke his God's name to induce healing? Was Elisha not aware that Naaman had way better rivers back home? For that matter, the Dead Sea is just south of the Jordan. Isn't there a rather large healing spa industry there?

It's one thing to open the garage and declare it cleaning day. It's a great step to call your best friend and say, "I am an alcoholic, and I need some help." It's wise to seek an alternate source of healing if you've got leprosy. But, that is all just more human doing. You're going to have to be willing to forget what you know and actually put some new things into practice. Your best thinking got you here. Only new thinking will get you out.

Naaman had some good advisors who quickly set about getting his ego calmed down. They reminded him that the point of this whole journey was to find an alternative cure to his disease, and despite the snobbery of the prophet Elisha, Naaman should at least give this advice a shot. I mean they were already right there close to the Jordan and everything.

Naaman went down to the Jordan and took a dip, seven of them to be exact. Done exactly as prescribed by Elisha. As he made the emergence from the final immersion his advisors knew that it was going to be a good day, and that their advice had potentially set them up for some really nice Christmas bonuses. This hardened general now had a baby's face. His willingness to forget everything he knew up until this point, and go for what seemed to be the less than rational option according to how he had viewed the world up until now was the ticket to his healing.

***

The public nature of my addiction and recovery has led to some privileged opportunities to sit down with folks who are struggling with their own addictions, and many who have decided to head to a treatment facility. Everybody is always curious about what they are going to experience, what rules they are going to have to follow—we addicts hate rules. When I give advice for making it through—because going in can feel like one is headed to Army Ranger boot camp—key phrase there is "feels like"—it's not. Part of the advice I often throw down is, short of committing a felony, do whatever they tell you to do. Heck, do it twice! If there is ever a time to follow some Jesus advice when He says, "If someone asks you to walk a mile with them, then walk two." Then it is when you are on the receiving end of wisdom of which you have not been previously privy. Wisdom that just might change your life.

If someone who has one more day of sobriety than you says to go out and stand on your head for thirty minutes a day, then do it. Who cares if it doesn't make any sense? Who cares if you look silly? It's only embarrassing, if you're embarrassed. If sobriety is what you are shooting for, then don't make it about ego or what you know. Just try it and see what happens. For the record, no one has ever coached me to stand on my head to maintain sobriety, but I promise I love my new life so much that if they did, I would.

We are not just talking sobriety stuff here either. If you want things in your life to be different, then you have to learn to think and be different. If a new diet can lead you to the body you want or provides a doctor-recommended alternative to the medicine you take, then maybe its time to be open to it, even if it's not full of foods you have previously enjoyed. If you are tired of being strapped for cash at the end of the month, then maybe it's time to rethink your relationship with money, and stop allowing it to be in charge of where it goes versus where you want it to go. If you want to reduce some of your anxiety, then maybe it's time to rid yourself of the preconceived stereotypes of a meditative practice and start breathing. If you want to change anything in your life—and you probably didn't pick up this book because everything is perfect—then maybe it is time to forget everything you know about it and make room for new, actionable information. Maybe it's time to stop your current human doing.

Naaman took a dip in the Jordan River. I threw out all those old college papers and the knowledge they represented. (My garage is clean now!) And, in rehab I made room for a whole new way of looking at life, and as a result I am sober, writing this book.

Be Still

One of the things I love about my faith community is that we have a lot of friends. Our friendships are not just limited to the folks that we gather with on a weekly basis, but they are spread out all around our geographical region, and even in foreign countries as far away as Ethiopia and as close as the Dominican Republic. We do life together. This means that we periodically get together, we learn from one another, and when one of us has a challenge like building a library for a bunch of kids, we all pitch in and get it done. But one of the best things that we do together is eat!

I am a foodie. This means I am always ready to try something strange or exotic on the chance that it pleasantly extends my flavor profile. It also means that for the everyday culinary experiences like coffee, I am always on the hunt for the perfect cup. Having friends in Ethiopia and the Dominican Republic has certainly been beneficial for my inner coffee connoisseur.

A few months ago I had the chance to be in the Dominican Republic and I was having an extremely important conversation with our friend, Tom, who originally introduced us to other friends there. This conversation was centered on what it took to pour the perfect cup of brew. The Dominican Republic is known for its extraordinary coffee. Many folks have coffee bushes growing right in their backyard. It doesn't get fresher than that. Every time I've been there I've made sure to swing by the grocery store and pick up a few pounds of their local brand to bring back with me so that I can recreate the majestic morning experience of the first taste. It has never worked. (Insert sad faced emoji here.) I wasn't sure what I was doing wrong. Was it the way I held my head when placing the grounds in the machine? Maybe the grounds didn't appreciate me serenading them with my sensational morning song? Or, was I even doing anything wrong? Was it the chemical tap water in the states, or the atmospheric pressure in my house? I knew Tom, a fellow foodie, would have the answer.

As we were sitting at the breakfast table, I made my inquiry and Tom said, "John, do you have one of those?" as he pointed to the stove behind us. He was pointing at an old school, stained, metal, stove-top Italian espresso maker. "Why no, I don't. I don't make my coffee with ancient technologies." I responded. He said, "Well you should. That's the secret to a great cup of Dominican coffee."

I was off to the races. I brought home my usual few pounds of Dominican beans, went to the store and got the required old school equipment, and the next day I was ready to replicate my mornings in the Dominican Republic. There was a slight learning curve in figuring out how to use this old fashioned contraption, but pretty soon the beautiful nectar was hot and ready for consumption. Turns out there is one more thing you have to do to pour the perfect cup of coffee. Probably the most obvious, but most important. You have to hold the cup still.

Hot! Ouch!

One of the most valuable things I have learned in the transformation from human doing to human being is that the same basic principles apply in order to pour a great life. You can be born into the right heredity, have the best alma maters, climb the most sturdy of ladders, and even pick the right faith community, but if you can't sit still, if you can't stop doing, then all those ingredients will never make it into a great life. They can even wind up causing you more pain than pleasure. You can also have a life where seemingly nothing has gone right for you. You could have been raised by wolves, still have to sound out the big words, fallen off the corporate ladder, and have nothing to do with those "hypocrites" of faith, but until you find the value in sitting still and purposely not human doing you'll never be steady enough to keep from spilling a great life out all over the place.

My mom and dad will attest that from the moment I was born I have been an "all in", type AAA personality. Sitting still has never been a thing for me. Why sit still when there is an appendage to fidget, a world to conquer, and only so many heart beats in which to do both?

As a child, it would take me hours to fall asleep as I would lie in the bed at night contemplating how to use the scrap wood in the back yard to build a bike repair empire, or imagining what my future life of world leader would would be like. Yes, there is an ego theme to every part of my life.

This busy mind led me right into an adult life that may have had different fantasies, but still the same effect on my constant need to keep moving, doing, and achieving. Sleeping was for the weak. Sitting still was for those who liked watching their futures fly away. I was a human doing personified. I was always moving and as a result, my cup was always shaking.

As the regular events of life unfolded, some pleasant and some not so pleasant, I took no time to process each event. Emotions were always ignored at the price of moving forward. Feelings were not to be felt, but rather to be generated and used as a means to an end. Over the years I begin to notice more and more times that emotions, particularly anger, would simply decide to surface unannounced. It would wreak it's seemingly temporary havoc, and then slink back to where it came from, a place where it seemed to always be a steady present energy within me.

I experienced a variety of other emotions too, which included the ones we all love the most like love, joy, happiness; but there were also the ever growing realities of fear, resentment, and sadness. The mind that was creating the thoughts, that were creating these emotions was never quiet. It was never still. Over time the easiest way to dull the mind and the unwanted feelings was simply to have a drink, or two, or three, or you get the point. While this book is written through the lens of an alcoholic, your human doing has probably found its own active and destructive ways of quieting the current unwanted thoughts and past emotional stressors.

***

So here I am walking into my first day of group therapy. I couldn't wait to get my Kumbaya on. I have no idea who these people are, and they have no idea who I am, but dawg gone it we are going to heal! By this description you can tell that my bravado was really covering for my nervousness. I sat in the most inconspicuous chair I could find in the counselor's office, and waited for the healing to begin.

Our counselor made her way into the office in a very calm, yet confident, in-charge kinda way. I could tell she was the type to get things done. She would help me get to the bottom of all this crazy residing in me. Heck, with her know how and my drive we might combine to make this the fastest healing in rehab history. I might even get to graduate early. Let's do this thing!

She sat down and proceeded to turn on some strange sounds for our supposed listening pleasure. The thing I found most odd was that she was playing these from a playlist on her phone. Who would have this kind of dull, boring, and ambiguous music available at a moments notice on their playlist? This stuff made elevator music feel like a Metallica concert—by the way I've unfortunately never been to one of those. Where was the pump you up music? Let's get this party started type of jam?

She then gave us our first set of instructions. We were to simply sit still. Breathe. And enjoy the calmness of the melodic notes for a few minutes. If there was going to be a time for a potential coup d'etat this was going to be it. Otherwise, we would all fall prey to the cult that this lady was attempting to induct us into. I glanced around the room in a last ditched attempt to make eye contact with one of my fellow inmates. Whom would I find that had that same panicked glimmer in their eye, signaling that they would join me in this harrowing escapade to freedom? Someone who would listen when I yelled, "I'll take her high, you go low!"

There was no one. It seemed that each of them had arrived just days before me. They were weak. They had already succumbed to the devilish wiles of this woman's deceptively calm mystique. I was now stuck listening to this music while sitting and doing absolutely nothing for eternity. Then her five minute timer went off!

***

One of the good things that we addicts have going for us is that we are the afore mentioned "all-in" people. Why have one drink when you can have ten? Makes perfect sense, right? Well, if you're an addict it does. If you can turn that same tenacity and overboard approach to life against the addiction, then chances of long-term survival skyrocket. I was determined to approach rehab with all the gusto that I had approached addiction. Whatever it took!

Every morning at breakfast we could pick up the schedule for the day. I was never sure why they were so committed to the deforestation of the Amazon since after about two days the schedule was never different. Routine, they say, is good for us. Looking at the schedule on the first day I noted quickly that there did not have to be an accounting for every minute of our time. There were several spots on the schedule where the event available was listed as "optional". Optional? Not for me! You only get one shot at hitting the playground bully in the nose and taking him down. Rehab was my punch in this addiction's nose, and nothing would be optional for me on the schedule. If it was available, then that meant that somebody somewhere farther down the road of recovery than me thought this might be helpful, and that meant I was going to give it a try. Punch the bully, and then keep kicking to keep him on the ground.

One of the events marked as optional was a word I didn't even know how to pronounce, much less what it could possibly be—Acudetox. Sounds like a party doesn't it?

I asked around a bit trying to figure out what I was getting myself into. Turns out that Acudetox is acupuncture for the detoxification of the body. Yes, the type of acupuncture that involves someone turning you into a human pin cushion. If I was going to stick with my nothing's-optional-and-anything-may-help attitude, then I was going to have to surrender to this new form of insanity too.

I arrived on time at the appointed hour. It would seem that others were aware of the need to get there early, because the place was already full of people sitting in chairs with their eyes closed, breathing heavily, with tiny needles sticking out of their ears. You read that right. Tiny needles sticking out of their ears. This was my big chance to run, but the very serious nurse lady saw me and before I knew it I was sitting in a chair waiting to be pierced.

My ears were properly swabbed with a sanitary wipe—at least there was a semblance that this process would not transmit any communicable diseases—and then the weirdness ensued. The nurse asked me to sit very still while she inserted the needles. She wouldn't have to ask me twice. Sitting still it is. I was taking no chances on a misplaced needle in my ear. As she gently poked each needle into its appropriate spot she would say things like, "And this one will connect with your joy." Who knew this would be all that it took to connect with my joy? Needless to say, I was a big time skeptic, but nothing was optional.

Be Still

A total of five needles were placed all along different points in each ear. I am so thankful that phones were not allowed in rehab, otherwise pictures would certainly circulate in the future of this most ridiculous moment in personal history. She then asked if I had ever meditated.

Another "non-optional" class that I had already attended was one on meditation. The Spiritual Life Director of the facility had led this monumentally boring event. A fifty-five minute lecture on the scientific benefits of meditation, and a five minute practice on how to do it. Simply put. Breathe, and notice it.

I asked the nurse, "That thing where you just focus on your breath?"

She said, "Yeah. Close your eyes and do that."

My head began to swirl with dread and anxiety. It had only taken her five minutes to get me all pinned up, and this was supposed to be an hour-long event. Testing the waters of meditation for five minutes in the other class had just about made me crazy. Now I had fifty-five minutes to sit here and do what? Feel my breath with pins sticking out of my ears? This wasn't detoxification, this was a study in new ways to get people to talk at C.I.A. blacksites.

"Okay." I calmed myself. "This is what it is. Just focus on your breath."

"John. John!"

I was coming to slowly, a bit dazed and confused. Where had I been taken? What was going on? Who is this crazy serious lady calling my name? Why is she dressed in nurse scrubs? Oh my! Do I still have all my organs, or are they already on a boat headed out to sea to the yacht of a biljillionaire who purchased one of my kidneys at a discounted rate?

"John, that session seemed to be exactly what the doctor ordered for you. You went really deep," said the serious nurse lady I was starting to remember from a few moments ago.

As I lifted my head I could feel the slimy connection from my mouth to my chest. What?! I've been sitting here drooling this

71

whole time? I thought you called yourself a nurse? Couldn't you have at least wiped a guy off?

I looked down at my watch and the full hour was up! In fact, most of my other fellow detainees had already exited the room. You have to understand, this was a miracle! Up until this moment I had not taken a nap in years, because I don't count passing out from too much alcohol ingestion a nap. If you could even call this a nap. It was more like having slipped into a coma. Napping for me had always been just one more time where trying to be still led to my mind racing about everything for which I was anxious, and then guilt for everything I should be doing instead of napping. I had given up on the concept of this type of rest a long time ago.

So what had just happened during this acudetox session? Whatever it was, it had to have been a fluke. I had two more sessions of this booked. I'd be ready the next time.

***

There's another story in the Old Testament part of the Bible. In a book called 1 Kings to be exact, in case you ever want to go and check it out. It's about a guy with the working title of Prophet, and his name was Elijah. He was the spiritual mentor and forerunner of the guy Elisha whom you met in the last chapter.

Prophets were folks who way back in the day had a special sensitivity to God. As God would reveal things to them, it was often not for their own sake, but rather for the sake of a nation who had lost their collective sensitivity to God. The prophets job was to take God's message to the nation, whether good or bad news. Most of the time since God was speaking to the prophet because the nation wasn't listening anymore, the news didn't usually turn out to be all that good. Again, Elijah was one of these prophets, and he was about to have another of what had already been many encounters with God. However, this one would not be for the sake of the nation he represented. This one was for him.

Right before this encounter, Elijah had a very busy few days. Propheteering can be a crazy busy career, especially when folks are not in the mood to really pay attention to what you have to say. It takes a little extra effort to get them to take notice. Elijah had just had what equated to an ancient U.F.C. match with another group of prophets, the prophets of a god named Baal. The thing is there's no such god that really exists. Baal was purely make-believe, and this was the point that Elijah was trying to get across. Getting his point across was quite the fireworks show, literally. The whole story involves a water soaked altar, self mutilation on the part of the prophets of Baal, Elijah's making fun of Baal for needing to relieve himself and not showing up to the contest, a pyrotechnics display of heavenly proportions, and ultimately the untimely and rather gory deaths of a bunch of folks who believed Baal was real. You should really check the story out sometime in 1 Kings chapter 18—just not right before bed.

The queen of Baal's prophets, Jezebel—yes, she's the reason you probably didn't name your daughter that, and my bad, if you did—was not a happy camper that four hundred of her top advisors were now in pieces down in the Kishon Valley. She immediately put out a death warrant on Elijah. He took off on the run.

Going on a run after an exhausting victory led Elijah to finally chill out in a cave for a few days. It was here where he would have his acudetox experience.

Elijah was depressed. He was down and out, the way we can all have a tendency to get after a hard-fought battle with life. The way you will feel should you ever end up in rehab. Win or lose, the process will still make you tired and demands rest. Unfortunately, most of us keep human doing rather than take the time to just Be Still. Whether Elijah was so tired he had no choice but to stop, so fearful he felt no options but to hide, or had just enough sense in his depressed state to freeze and rest, he managed to get still long enough to have a life changing encounter with God.

Over forty days had passed since Elijah had gone on the lam. He awoke in the morning following his first night in the cave to a voice that he had become familiar with in all his propheteering. It was the voice of God. What follows is my paraphrased version of this encounter.

God: "Elijah, what in the world are you doing in this cave? Why are you AWOL?"

Elijah: (Whining. Complaining. Whining. Complaining. Whining.)

God: "Leave the cave and go out to stand on the mountain."

Elijah: (In spite of all the whining and complaining he reluctantly follows suit.)

Boom! Massive windstorm slams the mountain! Rocks were ripped from the ground and Elijah probably pees his robe just a little bit.

God was not in the spectacular windstorm.

Crack! Huge rifts begin to form in the ground all around Elijah. The solid earth is rising up and down like the waves of the ocean. Elijah is now in need of a full on robe change.

God was not in the earthquake.

Sizzle! Flames burst forth all around. Fire engulfs the nearby trees and foliage. Elijah had wanted to die, but this was not exactly what he had in mind.

God was not in the fire.

Shhhh! The hush of a whisper spread over the landscape. Elijah covered his face. He now knew he was in the presence of God.

God had spoken in the whisper.

The instructions that followed next would snap Elijah out of his funk, and put him back firmly on the road of his life's calling. Most importantly, Elijah had just learned a lesson in always looking for satisfaction in the big moments and action of life. That's not where it's found. Most of life can be boring and mundane. Most of life is at the decibel level of a whisper and not that of a Metallica concert. It's in the stillness that

God speaks. It's in the calmness that we feel His presence. He created us as human beings not human doings.

***

The opportunity had arrived to debunk this myth of acudetox being a real thing. The myth of rest and stillness being something that a type AAA personality needed, or for that matter could even potentially achieve, had to be put to rest. The first appointment with Nurse Pinprick had to have been nothing more than an anomaly in the space time continuum. There was no way that the treatment had actually worked. I was headed into my second acudetox having had longer for my body to dissipate its chemical toxicity, a few nights of good sleep, and I was prepared to vindicate my prior weakness in adding data to the validity of things like acupuncture and meditation. As if being still could possibly be the answer to the turmoil of my soul. Whatever!

This time I got there a few minutes early like I had learned from the crowd before me in my first visit. This ensured the least perceptible seating position should the coma turned drooling phenomena repeat itself. That wasn't going to happen this time though. I had simply been in a weakened state on my first trip, and now I was aware of the game and had come prepared to prove the power of rest wrong.

After I sat down and got my sit bones all comfy in the chair's cushion, Nurse Pinprick came on over and started the process. This time she brought another chair over and asked me if I would like to put my feet up. Now I knew she was playing hardball, but if she thought for a moment that I was going down just because her tactics had changed, then she didn't realize just what kind of stubborn, egotistical super powers that I possess. I would not be denied.

"Sure, I'll take a chair," I said with a smidge of, "I know what you're up to" tone.

She let me place my feet up in the chair. A sanitary swab then made its way around my pinna—word of the day to look up if need be—and before long my love, joy, and peace that who would have ever thought resided in my ears were being connected to tiny little pins. With ten antennae sticking out of my head I was now poised to further detox from nine years of high exposure to poison. A.k.a. being tricked into rest.

I began the slow breathing in and out. This time I wouldn't just focus on my breath, because that may have been what took me down for the count last time. This time I had brought some problems to solve. Heaven knows there were plenty of those at this point in my life. How often do you get to sit and just think about how to fix your life? It was going to be a way better use of my time than relaxing and breathing.

"Mr. Smith. Mr. Smith! You can wake up now. Your session is over."

"What! Oh gross, what is this slime all over my chin?"

Maybe there was something to this acupuncture thing after all? Maybe just sitting, resting, and breathing could really be restorative to my soul. Maybe such an approach would do more than detox my body, maybe it would detox my life? More on that later, but for now know that I started playing around with this just noticing my breath concept. My breath; the first thing God ever gave me. Soon enough, others would notice that things were beginning to change. I was transforming from a human doing into a human being.

***

Nearly two weeks had gone by and five days a week it was exactly the same routine. Early breakfast—they don't let you sleep in at rehab. I guess they figure you've had enough unconscious time in your addictive life—big group lecture time, and then on to the healing factory that is smaller group therapy with your counselor. You remember her right? Confident, in-charge, cult leader who lets us start group time by rocking it out to worse than elevator music playlists.

On this particular groundhog day we all came in and took our habitual seats in the room. Our counselor entered. She hit play on her hypnotic tunes playlist, and I began the process of staring out over her shoulder, through the window, watching the morning sun dance along the waves of the Chesapeake Bay.

Beep. Beep. Beep.

The timer on her phone went off. Five minutes had passed and it was time to start swapping stories about the less than stellar ways we had all lived our lives up until now, and how it made us and others feel. But, before that started my counselor looked at me with an air of slight amazement.

She said, "John, I've got to say that I am really impressed, and quite frankly proud of you today."

It only takes one "I'm proud of you," to get my ego's attention.

"Yes ma'am, why is that?" I responded.

"Well, one of the things I've noticed about you is that you're always fidgeting. Most of all you always have at least one leg bouncing. You just sat through those five minutes without moving a muscle. You looked really relaxed. Good for you," she noted.

Oh, how I wish I would have had the ability to record that moment for my mom to see. She would be so proud, and recording it would be the only way to convince my mom at that time that such a miracle could transpire.

Maybe this was what was meant by the song writer turned King, David's, appeal to, "Be still and know that I am God." Maybe this was the secret to becoming a human being.

Stop Writing Fiction

A Saturday morning for a child in a small New Mexico oil town in the eighties consisted of watching early morning Bugs Bunny, and then going out and taking a look around the yard to see if he had dug through anywhere around the house because he had always taken a wrong turn at Albuquerque. That's how active my imagination always was. Wherever a good story left off, I could spend all kinds of time writing alternate endings. There was never any room for mystery in a story. If there was a gap in the plot line, then I had to make sure it had resolution. If there was a problem, then it must be solved. If something in a story hadn't been done, then my mind would do it. Exercising my human doing is one of the reasons I loved going to the library.

Every Saturday morning after cartoons and our subsequent rabbit hunt (truth is I don't know if it was every Saturday morning. You know how it is when you are telling a story about your childhood; It may not have been every, but it felt like it was) my mom would take my sister and me for a walk down to the little local library. I can still remember how small this place was. It only consisted of maybe ten loaded bookshelves in the center and then a few shelves lining the side walls. They did have a good collection of Nancy Drew novels though. The ultimate in mystery and mayhem. Every book was an opportunity to put all of my imaginative and problem solving skills into play and solve the enigma before the last page, beating Nancy Drew to the punch.

It would have been easy to be judged in that era for being a Nancy Drew fan versus a Hardy Boys fan in that I was a bustling young lad, but I had my reasons. I felt that Carolyn Keene was a more nuanced writer than Franklin W. Dixon. Nancy Drew was a more complex and realistic character than Frank and Joe Hardy. Pretty hefty analysis for a seven or eight year old. As I would later discover those authors were as fictitious as the characters and mysteries about which they were writing. They were nothing more than pseudonyms. That discovery is similar to my discovery in rehab that most of the stories that I had written about my life were fictitious. Plot lines I started, based in real life scenarios that were happening to or around me, and then my mind was off to the races to write the rest of the story—usually, a fictional story.

You see this is not my first book. It may be the first one that has ever actually made it into a readable format, but I have huge libraries full of fictional material. My human doing has been writing for a long time. These stories are all filed away in the library of my mind. There are stories about how I would become the greatest pastor the nations had ever seen with the largest church in human history, how I would some day replace Tom Brokaw as the suave and debonaire face that every American would see in their television sets delivering the important information that impacted their lives, or standing in front of the U.S. Capitol with my hand on the Bible held by a Supreme Court Justice accepting my fellow countrymen's call to lead them into a glorious future. I know. I know. You are commenting on my ego again.

I have also written many other types of fiction. I have stories of how I thought that crucial conversation with a coworker was going to go south. Stories of how I thought I would go bankrupt. How my car would break down on the two hundred mile road trip home. How I thought I may be dying of cancer. How my boss wanting to see me meant I was getting fired. How my wife may be deciding she doesn't love me anymore. How there is no way I could ever recover from alcoholism. How I would never actually be able to live a dream and write a book, because I don't have a good enough story to tell.

Shelves and shelves of fiction line my brain. Far more than that little library of my childhood could ever hope to hold. With every one of these fictional story lines, with every one of these thoughts that would never come to pass, there were emotions attached. Emotions of fear, anger, resentment, stress, doubt, sorrow, and despair. Emotions that there were never any reason to feel, because the stories that I was writing, that were making me feel them, were all fictitious. They were never going to happen. All of that pain for no reason. All those hours, all that money, and all those drinks to quell a self-inflicted pain, to calm a self-induced anxiety. Battling against storylines that were not real.

You may be like me and alcohol is your thing. Or, it could be food, porn, relationships, shopping, video games, work, gossip, binge watching, or an addiction to negative emotions. Yes, there is such a thing. No matter your poison, your go-to device for reducing the noise and pain of the fictional stories you are writing about yourself is also a device for canceling the ability to feel the love of God that is trying to break through to you. All of your doing is keeping you from becoming human.

Another problem is that using those devices as your life's coauthor is only causing you to write more fiction about yourself. It's time to lay the pen down or close the laptop. Your life is being written in a far grander way than you can ever imagine, by an Author known for solid and grandiose non-fiction stories. The kind where you live happily ever after. Not always easy in the here and now, but happily ever after.

***

Here's how bad this fictional story writing thing got. I can remember nights when I would come home having had an irritating day at work. I am an alcoholic so this would easily call for a few drinks in order to calm down enough and allow my mind to move into problem solving mode versus just pure irritation. Having achieved some false semblance of stability, I would then begin to purposely ruminate on the thing that was troubling me. The issue that had to have resolution. The mystery that had to be solved. It was not going to matter how many hours it took, how many present minutes with my family were robbed, or how many drinks I had to consume, whatever was bugging me had to be put to rest before the next work day. The problem with this approach is that in thinking about the problem I was also experiencing all the pain and irritation of the problem.

When I was younger I used to come to my mom and say, "Mom when I do this (and I'd show her some particular body movement) it hurts." My mom was an extremely wise woman and also very sarcastic–which is where I probably get my spiritual gift of sarcasm. She would say, "Then don't do that." Thanks Mom! Her lack of sensitivity aside, you have to admit that is some pretty good advice. If the doing is causing the pain, then stop doing! The problem is I had never learned that lesson. As an adult I was coming home every night and doing nothing more than figuratively moving whatever problem was emotionally hurting me. I was then writing stories as to how the problem could and should be handled, with every possible outcome of every character being considered. These further fictional movements caused me even more pain. Then I was self medicating in order not to feel the pain of the movement. It was a never-ending vicious cycle.

***

This whole scenario reminds me of another story that can be found in the bible. This time the story is in the New Testament book of Mark. It actually involves the most recognized character of the bible, Jesus.

Leading up to this story Jesus had been spending his day in much the same way he seemed to spend everyday of his life while on planet earth. Teaching about love and showing people how to love. Although it was all good work, it was work nonetheless. Spending that much time with broken people will wear you out. Ask my counselors. As the day drew to an end he told his disciples–the guys he had hand picked to be his immediate followers–to go load up the boat because they were going to head over to the other side of the lake. This would take most of the night and give him the opportunity for some snooze time.

The disciples came from various backgrounds, but most of them seemed to know their way around a boat and the water, and a few of them actually made their living on the lake as fishermen. Not long after they had gotten on the boat Jesus slipped back to the back and grabbed his favorite pillow before anybody else had the chance to claim it. The story only says cushion, not pillow, and I added the stuff about somebody else trying to claim it, just because this was a real life scenario, and we all know that in real life the best cushions go quick.

It wasn't long before the self-proclaimed Savior of the world was snoring away. I wonder if Jesus drooled too? I bet he did.

Now most likely the lake that the story is referring to is the Sea of Galilee. Located today in what we know as the modern state of Israel. A long time ago I had the chance to actually go out on a boat on the Sea of Galilee. Again, "sea" is a misleading name. It is a really big lake. While we were out there on the boat our guide was telling us something about how when the winds came out of the hills surrounding the lake in just the right way it could produce immediate and crazy storms even to this day. We didn't have smart phones back then, so I couldn't Google anything to see if he was telling us the truth, or just giving us a good story to help this bible story make more sense. Whatever the case may be, according to the bible story we are recounting here, sudden storms are in fact a thing on the Sea of Galilee. And, I guess every storm is sudden if you don't have a weather app that can keep you up-to-date on the hour by hour forecast.

A storm came up. Things were getting crazy quick. Waves were coming up and over the sides of the boat. The disciples hadn't even had time to put their life jackets on. Oh, wait. They didn't have those then. Even worse. More unwelcome water came into the boat and it didn't have anywhere to go. It was piling up in the bottom inch by inch. The disciples looked around at the situation, and it was not looking good. As we have already learned in this chapter, if you have a problem you are up against with an uncertain outcome, the best thing to do is speculate by writing fictional stories about the worst possible outcomes, and then panic! (Please note the spiritual gift of sarcasm leaking in there.)

That's exactly what they did. The biblical story doesn't tell us what the stories they were writing about this situation were, but being a great writer of stories in these type of situations myself, I bet I can make a stab at it.

I can guarantee there was one of them screaming, "We're all gonna die!" There is always one in every group screaming, "We're all gonna die!" I'm guessing in this case it was Peter. He was most often the overdramatic one of the bunch.

You know somebody was sitting there all curled up in the fetal position sucking their thumb, crying, and whimpering, "Please, make the bad storm stop."

Judas was certainly considering all his options of self preservation, which probably included snatching Jesus' cushion, turning it into a flotation device and jumping overboard leaving everyone else to deal with a potential capsizing.

Thomas was probably sitting over on the side with his eyes closed in deep denial that this was even happening, trying just to imagine his happy place.

Somebody finally got the bright idea to go wake up Jesus.

"The disciples woke him up, shouting, 'Teacher, don't you care that we are going to drown?'" (Mark 4:38b)

This didn't go exactly as they had planned though. Jesus was not too happy about having his sleep interrupted. He was enjoying just being. He was not in the mood to do anything. This was his nap time. Concern for drowning was not exactly at the top of the list for a guy who could walk on water.

Verse 39 of Mark 4 says, "When Jesus woke up, he rebuked the wind and said to the waves. 'Silence! Be still!'"

And wait a second. Let it soak in—no pun intended. The phrase, "Be still!" again.

Jesus seems to be piping hot at this moment. Storms come in life. Bad things happen that are out of our control. You can be an expert in your industry, but you don't control the economic seasons of your industry. You can eat an apple every day and go to the gym and still get cancer. You can never have had a ticket and be in a horrendous traffic accident. Bad things happen to good people. Bad things happen to bad people. Bad things happen. Storms are real. It's the stories we write about them that often determine the extent of the damage they can and will do to us.

All speculation aside, the disciples had certainly written a story about this storm. The story as reported earlier was, "We are going to drown." Heavy winds. Non-fiction. High waves. Non-fiction. Boat turned bathtub. Non-fiction. Sea sickness. Speculation. Drowning. Fiction!

What was Jesus' reaction to the disciples fictional story writing? Jesus was left with no option but to give the disciples a human "F" for fear on this creative writing experiment. Jesus wanted to give them a Jesus "F" on this assignment; a Jesus "F" stands for faith. The disciples had not chosen faith.

I wonder who was Jesus really talking to when he bellowed the words, "Be still!"?

Was it just for the wind and waves that Jesus was so dynamically giving this order, or was it for the disciples too? Could it be that when the waves get crazy and the problems big, the best advice is to sit down and be quiet? Don't pick up the pen and paper, don't open the laptop, don't start writing a story for your mind's library. Just be still. Just see how this thing plays out. Let things be, and let the one who said, "I Am.", write the next sentence.

I was in rehab, so I obviously hadn't learned to stop writing stories yet.

***

My mom always talks about how she began praying when we were very young for the future spouses of both myself and my sister. For my sister it was the typical, "God, please give her somebody amazing." For me it was probably more along the lines, "Dear God, please just let there be someone, because whoever it is will achieve the status of sainthood by just deciding to deal with him." Regardless of motive, it worked. I landed Mrs. Amazing.

One of the signs of her amazingness is the way she loved me through the nine years of my active addiction. Like all addicts, I left those around me often feeling lonely, afraid, and hurt, but in spite of that I was fortunate enough—because she chose love—to be one of the only people in rehab who was not concerned about losing their relationship with their spouse. Mrs. Amazing was going to be there when I got out, and one of the strongest signs of that was she was there on family weekend.

Addiction, like every disease is a family and friend thing. It's not just the addict who suffers. By the way, not to be judgmental, but just to add some awareness, whatever you're struggling with, however your human doing is manifesting itself, it is affecting your family and friends too. Good rehab facilities often offer a weekend where spouses can come join the fun, and sit with professional counselors both privately and with their spouse. It was in such a session where I would have to confront what my years of fictional story writing had been doing to my psyche and my soul.

If you would have asked me before this experience, I would have told you that my gift of story writing was a positive thing. I would have said that it gave me the ability to approach a problem from all the angles. It gave me the opportunity to be prepared for any situation. It ensured that no detail would be left undone and no danger sign undetected. It guaranteed that I would always have a plan of action no matter what the scenario.

All it really ever did was cause me to get mad at people who had never even done or said anything to me yet. I would be thinking about a crucial conversation I needed to have with someone, imagining their worst response possible—all in the name of being prepared for it—and then getting all heated in my head at the fictional words I had just put in their mouth. You would think that putting oneself through such a scenario is some type of psychosis, but from talking with every other human doing I know, it seems to be a thing we all do. It is fictional story writing and it's killing us one bad emotion at a time.

I would also find myself worried about make-believe events. Events that I have mentioned earlier like bankruptcy, car bursting into flames, and kids becoming homeless because we couldn't afford to send them to college. These stories helped me plan so that I could avoid such horrendous scenarios. Right? No. They had nothing to do with planning. They were the inventions of a mind that wants to control a world that it has no control over.

While my wife and I were sitting with our family counselor, the counselor was trying to explain to me this whole fictional story concept. I was making the argument that writing these stories helped me be prepared, and that they helped me to be a good husband and provider by always having a plan. And then she said it. The thing that would finally make it all click.

"John, it's fine to plan for the future. Just don't live in it. That's where all the stress resides."

She was exactly right. I was always living in some anxious story that I was writing about my future, or in an already written story of regret about my past. I was never able to just enjoy the here and now. I had always been one of those kids who was getting strapped into an amazing ride at the amusement park, and talking about how I couldn't wait to get off this ride to go to the roller coaster. If I was in the third grade, I couldn't wait to get to the fourth. In high school I knew that things wouldn't get awesome until college. And on and on it goes. I don't know how many times I heard my mom say, "John, just enjoy this moment. You won't have it forever." I never learned to do it as a kid, and I hadn't learned it as an adult either.

Since that time I have discovered the quote by Fulton Oursler, "Many of us crucify ourselves between two thieves - regret for the past and fear for the future."

Crucifixion was definitely starting to feel like what I had experienced in all of these years of ignoring the present and writing fictional stories about the future.

Thankfully, life has a way of teaching us these lessons, and then giving us plenty of opportunities to put them into practice. Mine would come just a few weeks out of rehab.

***

You might imagine that I should have been living in ecstatic joy over the fact that I had just spent 28 days in rehab, was now attending a six week outpatient program, and through it all still got to keep my job at a church. However, ecstatic joy was not what I was experiencing. I confess my emotional state was not as bad as it was when I had been drinking, but there was still a whole lot of anxiety and fear that were coauthoring stories in my mind.

I kept living with the intensity of wondering when the shoe would finally drop. When I would have the conversation with my pastor that said, "Well, John, we're glad you made it through rehab, but after further consideration the staff doesn't really feel as if they can follow your leadership anymore, so I am going to have to try and find someone else." If you knew my pastor you would know how insane this fictional story was. However, that novel still had a place in my library.

It was intensified when I was on the phone with my pastor one day while I was pacing through the church's atrium. Right before I had left for rehab, one of our key staff positions had been vacated, and with my return it was time to get the ball rolling in looking to fill the role. This assignment was typically in my lane and one of my responsibilities. This was something I was supposed to be human doing. I was completely consumed by fear when in this phone conversation with my pastor he informed me that he wanted one of my colleagues to take over this very important personnel search. My colleague was more than qualified and capable of doing this job well, but what did this mean? Was this the first step for me toward the final one of my time being employed here? Was I going to be "demoted" to a different role? Even worse, would I retain this role as an emperor with no clothes? The stories started to be written faster than ever before.

I did have a new commitment in place of being honest about my emotional state when things were off kilter. This conversation had definitely caused that to be the case. I told my pastor in the conversation that I was feeling a bit insecure about his decision, and to that he responded directly, "John, if I wanted you gone, then you'd be gone." That may sound a bit harsh, but to the healing addicts mind it's exactly what and how it needed to be said. It was a direct order to stop writing stories and just learn to live with what is. Do you think I listened? Nope!

Not long after that a candidate rolled into town. One who was highly qualified way above the position for which they were being considered. In fact, not only could they do the job we were looking at them for, but they'd probably be darn good at the potentiality of my job as well. Guess who started writing stories? Do I even need to tell you what kind of novels I was penning this time?

The breakthrough came when the whole staff got together to meet and spend time with the potential candidate at a private staff home that sat along a beautiful river. It should have been a fun day, but for a master writer of fictional horror it was anything but. While everyone was laughing, eating hot dogs, jumping in the water, story telling, throwing horseshoes, and being human, I was fake smiling and brooding over what I just knew was about to happen to me and my position. The writer in my head was cranking out words at a rate that if they were being typed the keyboard being used would catch on fire. The energy in me was getting crazy. I was feeling the uncontrollable urge to make sure I picked up a drink after this little shin dig.

I walked out into the river which was very shallow at the time, and decided to take a walk downstream away from everyone. There was really only one way out of this that I could see. I was going to have to wake Him up.

"Jesus, don't you care that I am going to drown?"

To my surprise he wasn't upset. He simply said, "Peace, Be Still."

I sat down—still—on the river bank that day with my feet in the cool water and decided that it no longer served me to read the old stories of regret that were on the shelves of my mind's library. I decided that I would start using the tools I had learned in rehab to prevent me from human doing and writing fictional stories about the future, and for this moment I would just enjoy the beauty. The beauty that was that calm and peaceful river.

It wouldn't be easy. And it won't be for you either. But, I decided from that point on I would practice, practice, practice, until I could see my problem, issue, or anxiety floating toward me, and just like the limbs of debris floating down the river I would let them pass right on by. I wouldn't chase them any longer. I wouldn't go do. I would just be still with Jesus.

Take Out the Trash

Even as I am writing this it is still weeks away, but the energy of this yearly phenomenon is already starting to absorb all the oxygen in and around the church office. Staff is planning, spending, recruiting volunteers, and pulling out all the stops. This is an all hands on deck type of event for church life. It really doesn't matter what denomination, background, or size of church. It is a phenomenon that will cause church attendance to skyrocket in such a way that if its a church with under a hundred people normally it is now in the hundreds, if a church runs hundreds it has over a thousand, and if it is normally over a thousand it will officially move into a mega church, over 2,000 people category. You may not even go to a church or like church, but if you did, have, or will, it is most likely to be on this day—Easter!

Why do people turn out in droves for this day? People who otherwise couldn't care less about the whole religious scene make an appearance in their new swag. Is it that? A chance to show off the latest acquisition of the new spring line? It can't just be for a bunny and some eggs stuffed with really gross marshmallows covered in sugar? Being a big fan of jelly beans, you might be able to convince me that they have something to do with it, but not enough to warrant such an all out upheaval of that many folks' weekend party going, sports watching, yard manicuring schedules, all to go to church.

There has to be something more than that, and although most other phenomenons in life have multiple factors feeding into their sustainability, I tend to think the reason this one is such a big deal is pretty simple. It celebrates the story of someone who rose again from the dead!

Who wouldn't want to celebrate that?

It's one thing to hear a story of how someone was pulled out of the rubble of an earthquake alive after days of being trapped. How someone with cancer went into surgery only to have the doctor discover that the tumor was no longer there. Maybe how a check showed up in the mail for the exact amount needed just before foreclosure. But, resurrection? Somebody who was dead and then comes back to life? That's not a story you get to hear everyday. That's the ultimate comeback!

So people come year after year to see and hear the same story told in a myriad of different creative ways. They come to be reminded of the miracle. Whether they choose to believe the story or not, they find a ray of hope in the idea of someone making such a dramatic comeback as that of a resurrection. If there is even the slightest inkling that something like that is possible, then maybe that means there is hope for their relationship, finances, health, or general happiness.

Quite frankly it's always been my favorite story. As a kid, I loved Christmas because Santa brings toys and candy; the Easter Bunny just brings candy. But in terms of the story itself, even as a kid, I knew a re-emergence from the dead was way more exciting than the birth of a baby. As an adult, I found that the story really did give me hope. It wasn't until I was able to rectify intellectually that such a possibility even existed, that I was able to become a truly devoted follower of Jesus. I realized even in my alcoholism that if resurrection was possible then I might be able to overcome this disease too.

The resurrection story leads to hope. It says that no matter what our human doing has done or what has been done to us that it cannot destroy our God created human being. That's why we celebrate it! There is one problem with this resurrection story. A problem that I had never really given enough attention until I found myself in rehab. A problem that not too many people ever take the time to really think about, and thus they continue to live with a whole lot of fear, resentment, and stress. Here's the problem.

There is no resurrection without a crucifixion.

Did you hear that? You can't come back to life again without having been dead first. Something tells me that if some pharmaceutical company came up with a pill tomorrow that could bring the dead back to life, they would still never be able to bring it far enough along in the test process to get it to public trial. Why? Well, to find out if it worked, you would have to have volunteers willing to die first. Sane people who are allowed to participate in such pharmaceutical tests would not be lining up to take the pill. No, thank you!

And I know some of you are saying, "Well, you could just use the corpses of already dead people." And if that is you, then you're messing up my analogy, making me rewrite the last brilliant paragraph, and missing the bigger point. Ain't nobody wants to die to find out if they can be resurrected.

And in Jesus' case, it's not just that he was dead, but rather how he got that way. Crucifixion was one of the cruelest and most graphic forms of execution that humankind has ever thought up. I have not taken the time to tell you some of the gross things I had to encounter while witnessing people who were detoxing from opioids and heroin while in rehab, so I'll continue to keep this a vomit free zone by sparring you the details of crucifixion here. There are movies galore available for further research into the matter, but suffice it to say that it was awful. No one would ever want to go through that. But! There is no resurrection without a crucifixion.

***

I know that somewhere in the past I had to have seen them before. At one point, before I even recognized that I was an alcoholic, I sat down with a pastor friend who I knew was a recovering alcoholic. I told him that I thought I drank too much. He gave me a copy of Alcoholics Anonymous' Big Book. I read it. I know they are in there. I had to have seen them. But now they were glaring at me in big letters emblazoned on a massive banner in the front of the main meeting room. Now I really saw them. I didn't want to see them. In rehab they didn't care if you wanted to see them or not. You were going to see them. They would be repeated over and over again during your 28 day stay. You were expected to say them over and over again, even though they made you very, very scared. They were just words, but looking at them was my version of having to stare at a cross on which I was to be emotionally crucified. Here are the ones that would cause the most pain. The ones that would lead to death.

Step 4: Made a searching and fearless moral inventory of ourselves.

Step 5: Admitted to God, to ourselves, and to another human being the exact nature of our wrongs.

Step 8: Made a list of all persons we had harmed, and became willing to make amends to them all.

Step 9: Made direct amends to such people wherever possible, except when to do so would injure them or others.

Let me make this a little more plain. Think back on every thing you've ever done wrong. Every way that you have hurt somebody, whether they know about it or not. Write it down. Go get a safety deposit box from a high security bank in Switzerland. Fly over and place that list in the box. Throw the key into any random enormous body of water. You're done. You're healed.

Okay, so maybe I made up the part about the safety deposit box and everything that followed. That's what I was hoping that it said, or at least thinking about doing.

Back to writing down all the ways you've hurt folks, and then going directly to them—if it's not going to hurt them more—and try and do whatever it takes to make it right. Not just say the obligatory, "Sorry." Do what you can to make it right. Sound like fun to you, or more like an emotional and psychological crucifixion?

There is no resurrection without a crucifixion.

Let's make something really clear about this process. We are not talking about doing it in order that you can achieve spiritual salvation or forgiveness from an all loving heavenly Father. We're talking about doing it so that you can put aside your human doing and become a human being. We're talking about doing it so that you can find peace.

***

Back in the day when I was a hip and happening bachelor—as you can tell by that statement I was never hip and happening—I was also the student pastor of a church out in Texas. I've introduced you already to Tally, my best friend. We have always been able to talk each other into the craziest of scenarios like last minute flights to Key West, and backing up all the way down a major road in order to get the chance to meet our favorite politician. Eventually, we are going to ride a horse on a boat. Don't ask. There is a song. This is the kind of stuff best friends do. At this particular time in our life I was able to talk him into coming down to Texas from Virginia to be the summer intern for our student ministry.

I had one of those early ministry gigs where they can get away with not paying you as much by giving you a place to live. I can't complain though. I was a bachelor with "free" housing in a pretty good sized place. I was saving for a ring for my girl. I'll take it! Meanwhile, Tally, you can just stay with me for the summer.

I don't remember a lot about that summer—because I am old and that was a long time ago—but I still have a very clear picture of what the front dining room of the house looked like midway through the summer. It was stacked with over twenty something, filled to capacity, black garbage bags. It was all our garbage. Not sure how long it had taken to accumulate that many bags for only two guys, but judging by my olfactory memory a few of the bags on the bottom had to have been there for some time.

How did it get like that? We were bachelors, but the dumpster was also a long way away. The regular trash truck didn't pick up at the actual house, because the house was attached to the church property. I guess since the church did not have to pay property taxes the county had decided that whoever was in the house should just throw their trash in the church dumpster. One less stop for the trash truck. Did I mention that the dumpster was a long way away? It was at least a good hundred and fifty yards.

Don't judge us! That's a long way off when the other option is the dining room.

Isn't that how life slowly builds up on us too? We start out in what seems like a pretty nice place to live. Early on, dealing with the garbage is easy enough. You hit your sibling, and mom and dad make you throw it in the trash can with a less than meaningful apology. You look off the paper of a fellow student for that one answer you just can't seem to recall, and now people think you're smarter than you are. Throw it in the trash. It will be awhile before that one starts to rot.

Then as you get older, people start coming over to your life with their trash and together you create even more trash. Dad, who has always felt less than because of that time he missed the game winning catch is going to make up for it by ensuring that you become an NFL all-star. You resent him for all the yelling, screaming, and embarrassment at games along with further backyard practices, but just throw it in the trash. It's no big deal. The young man you are dating thinks he has too much testosterone for one girl to handle, so he dates a few on the side to spread the love. Just throw the stinky pain of that fish in the trash. You'll move on. There are more fish in the sea.

Compromise after compromise, hurt after hurt, human doing piled on human doing, and it all starts to stink after awhile. The trash is starting to stack up a bit, which means it's going to be a bit of a chore to take it out. The simple solution is air freshener. Enjoy a piece of comfort cake. That was good! I believe I'll start doing that whenever I smell the smell. Veg out on the couch and watch crazy hours of television. At least the garbage is in the other room. There's a little room left on the credit card for those designer shoes. Who knows? Maybe that will inspire me to put them on and take a walk to the dumpster. Why not get a little drunk? The smell of alcohol is way better than the trash.

Life moves on and the trash piles up. Then come the snakes.

***

Now don't go skipping this part just because there has been a mention of snakes. I happen to be down with the little slithery suckers, but by now you have learned that I have issues.

I bring up the snakes part, because of a story I heard a guy—we will call him Bill for the sake of the next few paragraphs—tell in a support group that I hang out in for alcoholics. Bill was talking in regards to those hideous steps that I referred to earlier. The ones that call for you to pay attention to how you have hurt people in the past, and then step up to the plate and make account for it. The ones that say you should own your stuff.

Bill was referring to the snakes in his head being all the crazy thoughts that sometimes start to shoot through those neural pathways of the brain. The crazy, bad fictional stories that we write to fill in the blanks of our outer life's circumstances. We have already mentioned how every thought becomes an emotion. This means when our brain fires off a thought, our body fires off chemicals that lead to us having a real in the gut, neck, shoulders, head, feeling, about that thought. That emotion is the energy that throws us into action. Negative thought, negative emotion, and then negative action, leads to a negative life. I guess this is the reason guys like Paul, who was an early church leader said, "But let God transform you into a new person by changing the way you think." (Romans 12:2b)

Bill was saying that what he had learned over time was that snakes in his head were a clear indication of a deeper issue at play. Now follow along here. The rest of this could be a bit stomach turning for some, but better to have your stomach turned because of an analogy that isn't quite apropos, then to keep having it turned because of negative emotions.

Snakes only show up when there are rats, and rats show up because the trash has not been taken out. You can begin to get rid of the crazy thoughts when you begin to get rid of the trash.

There is no resurrection without a crucifixion.

So much of my emotional misery during nine years of active alcohol addiction was due to the secrets that I was keeping. The things that I was hiding. One of the truths that I had a counselor teach me was that when what you believe does not line up with your behavior, then your self esteem goes down the toilet. Mine had been in the sewer for a long time.

We believe life's not all about money and things; that people are the most important. Then we max out our credit cards and bury our face in our phones over dinner. We believe nurturing our bodies with food that comes from the earth is better for us and the environment we have been given dominion over, but we open the plastic wrap of a Twinkie and have a midday snack. I believed one probably shouldn't go through life intoxicated, and yet I drank way too much on a daily basis. That kind of trash leads to a messed up mind, and a messed up mind leads to a messed up life.

James, who was the brother of Jesus, wrote a letter to his Jewish friends who had become followers of Jesus. It's found in the New Testament of the bible, and they got real creative with the title of the letter or book. It's called, James. In it, James told his friends, "Confess your sins (faults) to each other and pray for each other so that you may be healed." (James 5:16a) This type of confession has nothing to do with any theological saving, it's about psychological wholeness. This is why so many who have become followers of Jesus and have felt the forgiveness of God still don't experience the subsequent love, joy, and peace that they assume is to follow. They may be "good with God," but they are still resentful toward their parents, hiding their addiction, covering up the affair, and in general leading a double life. Coming straight is about being able to look your fellow human being in the eye, and when they look back, you know they are seeing who and what you really are. A human being. No trash. No hiding. No secrets. No snakes.

I hated the words on that banner in front of that rehab meeting room. The words telling me that I would have to list the ways I had faulted others and then go and make it right with them. They were similar to words that I had read in the bible my entire life. I had come to understand there was only one thing I could do to get rid of the snakes. Take out the trash. Suffer a crucifixion.

***

Not long after getting out of rehab I was hanging out at one of these support groups. I met a super great guy named Howard—that's not really his name, but you get the point. We got to talking and he could tell that I had a lot of trash in the dining room of my soul that had not been taken out. He wasn't pushy or judgemental in anyway. He had told his story to the group earlier and he too once had a lot of trash removal that was necessary. He mentioned to me that he would be more than happy to help me get mine out to the dumpster. He said helping other people take out their trash was his way of reminding himself to keep his own house clean. He gave me his number and asked me to give him a call when I was ready. I didn't want to end up back in rehab. I gave him a call that night.

It's a total misnomer to believe that addicts are the only ones that need to go through this process. Remember this is a book about transformation from human doing to human being and what everybody has to go through to get there. Learning the importance of this trash removal process may be the difference between the life you are living emotionally and the one you want to. The difference between doing and being.

There is no resurrection without a crucifixion.

When you get to the point of self realization that built up trash is part of your challenge, and that you are going to have to do something about it—that will feel akin to an emotional crucifixion—then know that you are not going to want to be alone. This becomes the important role of a close friend that you know who has been through a similar process and can keep confidences, a spiritual leader in your life, counselor, or random gal or guy you met at a group like the one I was attending.

Someone who has been through the trash removal process themselves will best be able to guide you through your own. There are all kinds of nuances to be aware of like what to tell about past misadventures and misgivings, how much to tell, whom to tell it to, when to tell it, and how to go about rectifying hurt and pain caused to others if possible. You're gonna need some outside wisdom and support for this, and there are way more people out there ready to be with you through this process than you can possibly imagine. They are amazing people!

Howard and I started meeting in his finished basement so that our conversations would be completely confidential. He began guiding me through this process. It hurt! That's how crucifixions feel. Trash is smelly and heavy. But, over the course of some gut wrenching talks and visiting some painful emotional places, we were able to develop a plan of action to finally get my soul to a place I would be happy for others to come, see, and visit.

I knew the first bag of trash that had to be carried out, and the first nail I would have to suffer.

***

A couple of months had passed, and I had already started having many necessary conversations with the people whom I had affected during my life and active addiction years. There was one conversation that I had yet to have. It was not that I was putting it off, or that it was going to be particularly hard to have. I already knew what this person's response was going to be—or so I had written the story. The part of the story that I had written correctly was that they were going to be more than forgiving of what I had done to them. They already behaved in a way toward me that made that clear. The part that I had not written correctly is what I had actually done to them, and how it had affected them and me.

I didn't schedule the conversation. This is an individual that I see on a very regular basis, so I thought I would just wait until the conversation made itself available to me. This patience and timing thing was something I was also learning in this new state called human being. Everything does not have to happen right now it turns out. There is such a thing as delayed gratification. Not every present life gives us has to be perfectly wrapped up in a bow.

The other side of the table was were I was sitting the last time. That was when I had committed the crime. Just months earlier I had been sitting in that other chair when I did the thing that I would regret the very most during my entire addictive cycle. It's the place where I was sitting when someone who loved me was going to actually be giving me the chance to get the help that I had so often dreamed about being able to get. It's the place where my pastor, Drew, asked the infamous question that I had been hiding from for nine years. The question that if answered truthfully could lead to my freedom, and if answered falsely, my eventual demise.

"John, have you been drinking again?"

"No." I answered falsely. I lied.

The moment I said it, I felt as if I had just been hit by an emotional freight train. As an addict I have told a whole lot of fibs in my time. I can't make it to your funeral great grandpa. I've got too much to do this weekend to make the trip. I was going to drink. I cannot make that hospital visit right now. I'm in a meeting. I was drunk in a bar. I can't come in today. I'm sick. It was called a hangover. Yes, I had told a lot of lies over the years, but this one was my big kahuna. I would think about this lie I had said to this man every day of rehab, and every day up until this conversation months later.

The moment had now come. I shared with my pastor that I had lied to him that day. Would you believe he wasn't shocked? I shared with him the depth of anguish that this lie had brought upon me. I told him that I was truly sorry. I shared with him how having lied to him that day was the worst thing I felt I had done in all of my human doing. What he shared next would tell me it wasn't.

With tears in his eyes he said, "John, the hardest thing for me in all this is that I was afraid I could lose a friend. That a wife could lose a husband, and that three beautiful kids could lose a father. You are one of the greatest ministry partners that I have ever had, and I didn't want to lose you. I love you."

Even as I type these words I am seeing them through the lens of tears. That was the worst thing I had ever done. Not the lie. The worst thing I had ever done was not realize how much I was loved.

I am loved by my wife. I am loved by my kids. I am loved by Mom and Dad. I am loved by my sister. I am loved by my best friend. I am loved by my pastor. I am loved by my staff. I am loved by my church. I am loved by my community. Everywhere I go I am loved, because I am loved by God!

The greatest atrocity that you may be committing in your life right now is not realizing just how amazingly loved you are. You may have an incredible support system around you like myself, or you may be surrounded by broken and strained relationships. No matter, you too are loved by God! He resurrected His Son to prove it. You may not be reaping the benefits of that love because some trash is in the way.

It's time to take the trash out. It's time to make your own list. It's time to find a friend or trusted counselor that will non-judgementally guide you through your list of faults and coach you on how to work toward amends. It's time to go through the pain of a crucifixion. It's time to discover and feel just how loved you really are.

Without a crucifixion we would never know that there is a God who loves us so much that He will resurrect us.

Breathe on Purpose

This is going to be sooooo boring! That was the thought that hit me like a ton of bricks while I was sitting there on the workout bench of the weight room while in rehab. What was I possibly going to do in a sober life with all this new time I would have on my hands since I wasn't spending it drinking? Boredom is one of the reasons I had to drink in the first place.

In recovery there is an acronym we like to throw around called H.A.L.T. It stands for hungry, angry, lonely, or tired. It's a word to think about when the emotional pull toward our substance of choice is manifesting itself, and in my case saying, "Drink! Drink! Drink!" It's designed to make us consider whether or not we are experiencing any of those four things: hunger, anger, loneliness, or just tired. Those things are often triggers for our subsequent destructive behaviors. For me it is more like B.A.L.T. My version stands for bored, angry, lonely, or tired. I know. It's not as catchy and it doesn't make as much sense, but it works for me. These are a few of my trigger points. Things that can set me down the path of bar hopping and helping to build my core into a keg—that's shorthand for beer belly.

It's not just we known addicts that have these trigger points. Every human doing does. The physical, emotional, or psychological circumstances that lead us to make decisions like eating a piece of death by chocolate, or the better choice of putting on our should-be-banned spandex and heading to the gym. The decisions of human doing or human being. The thoughts we choose about life's sprinkles and storms that lead us to feel and then act. The subtle and sizable circumstances that life hands us that will either turn us into the best version of our created image, or lead us to a self destructive end. Growing in personal awareness is the art of identifying these triggers for what they are, and learning how to navigate them when they come knocking.

So bored is a big one for me—or at least it use to be. I've always liked to be where the action is. My ego likes to be the center of attention. Game day is my jam. Let's move! Let's go!

Boring leads to bars and beers. There's no doing in boring. My mind has to do something so it takes me to a secret life. Not a secret life of things needing to be confessed, but one like the life of Walter Mitty.

In present times, I know that when I mention Walter Mitty most folks probably started thinking of a B movie starring Ben Stiller a few years ago. Actually, I prefer the original story "The Secret Life of Walter Mitty" as written by James Thurber back in 1939.

Here's a comedic yarn about your average Joe, or in this case Walter, living out an ordinary day as chauffeur extraordinaire to his wife. She's got errands and he's got the car keys. I'm sure that when he was a little boy he wasn't thinking this was how life was going to turn out. Oh well, at least he's still got that boyhood imagination going for him.

Set against the backdrop of every environment that Walter finds himself on this average day are things that trigger his imagination to go to wild and fantastic places. In each of his self-created storylines he becomes the hero of the moment, whether it be as a Navy boat pilot, secret assassin, or in his final tragic scene as a martyr bravely facing down the firing squad as he defiantly smokes his last cigarette. If not a lion heart in real life, then his renowned cannot be denied on his own head. The story is so poignant because there are so many of us that can identify with Walter's plight. It's what Henry David Thoreau was referring to in Walden when he said, "The mass of men lead lives of quiet desperation." And ladies, I don't know why he left you gals out of the quote, because I know that it can and does equally apply. Few people really like the boring or mundane. Like the great philosophers of Loverboy say, "Everybody's Workin' for the Weekend." Waiting for the action.

My type triple AAA personality was caught in the endless cycle of go, go, go, do, do, do, and when I didn't have anywhere to go or anything to do, I would go to the bar. Every new, big challenge I believed would rescue me from my addiction, but eventually all my going just devolved into drinking more beer.

Now what I was learning in rehab was that if I wanted to get well, if I wanted to stop drinking, my life was going to become what seemed to my addicts mind to be a life that was a lot more boring. It would have to be a life of more being and less doing.

***

In an earlier chapter I took a shot at a guy named Peter, he was a follower of Jesus, otherwise known as one of the disciples. The shot was that I have always felt him to be the rather overdramatic type. The overdramatic person is somebody that has an addiction to the drama, or always being in the center of it. The overdramatic person can inflate any situation by writing an amazing fictional story of personal grandeur or potential doom. The behind their back chatter at the water cooler must be about whether they will be the one who gets the pink slip to which the boss has been alluding. The pain in their elbow is some type of debilitating cancer. This night at karaoke will be the one where the world's top music producer will hear their world class talent and sign them to a lifetime, multi-billion dollar contract. You know the type. Truth is, I am the type. Guess that's why I identify more with Peter than I want to admit.

Whenever Peter shows up in the story of Jesus you know things are about to get exciting. He could be having what I call an "AHA" moment in realizing that Jesus may be more than just your average miracle worker; he could be getting ready to jump out of the boat to go make his debut as water walker turned panicked deep sea diver, or he may be playing samurai with his sword and lopping off ears with less than precision type accuracy.

It's the final, normal night with Jesus, if there ever was such a thing. Jesus and his disciples are celebrating one of their cultures most important holidays, the Feast of the Passover.

Unlike his unassuming disciples, Jesus realizes the gravity of this evening. It would be the last supper he would have with them before his resurrection.

At one point in the evening the topic of betrayal pops up, and things take a turn toward the more serious. Everybody wants to know who is involved in this conspiracy and how it's going to go down. It's soon revealed that Judas—the name which has become synonymous with deception—will be the one to betray Jesus, and he hightails it toward the door to go do his treacherous deed.

With that out of the way, Jesus has his final crew in the room. They are not going to be with him all the way to the cross. The cross is a lonely place. Like walking through the doors of rehab, one can only experience this alone. However, the plan for this rag tag team of Jesus followers was not over yet, not by a long shot. They were going to need what Jesus was about to unpack over the course of the next few minutes for their lives going forward. A person's final words are often considered to be some of their most important. Jesus knew the gravity of this moment, so the words which he would offer would summarize and emphasize the guiding principles for which he had spent his life. Or should it be said, THE guiding truth for which He had spent His life.

In a book of the New Testament called John—named that because John, one of Jesus' followers in the room that night, is the one who wrote it—Jesus begins these pivotal minutes with a bunch of Jesus talk. Jesus talk is the stuff that mystery is made of. Jesus understood the world in a way that his followers did not and still don't. He could see the world of the unseen and the not yet known. When he would talk of these things that he often referred to as kingdom things, people would just scratch their heads and seem to say, "Hey, look. Could I just get my sight back?" His disciples caught on sometimes, but more often than not they too would just wait for the talk to return to something they could understand before reengaging a mindful presence with Jesus.

Jesus started this final chat with some Jesus talk about going places they couldn't go, and then he returns to some subject matter that they could hopefully wrap their heads around. They had better be able to, because what was about to be said was a drop the mic type moment. It was the most profound piece of art in the gallery. Attention must be paid.

Jesus says, "So now I am giving you a new commandment: Love each other. Just as I have loved you, you should love each other. Your love for one another will prove to the world that your are my disciples." (John 13:34-35)

Boom! There it is. The cornerstone, Mona Lisa, Nobel Prize winning, poet laureate, earth shattering truth that humanity has been missing since the beginning of time! Love each other, Jesus says.

While probably scratching his head in a Neanderthal type way, Peter—in my version of the moment—replies, "Uh, Jesus. You said something about going somewhere. Where exactly are you going again? I missed that part. Could you repeat it?"

Poor Peter.

I've often wondered whom Jesus has done that little side to side head shake with more. You know the one you do when you've tried real hard to explain something to someone, and they are just not getting it. I wonder if Jesus did that more with Peter, than he has with me? My mom would probably say he has done it more with me.

Jesus doesn't even go back and try to explain to Peter that he has missed the most important point. He realizes that Peter isn't ready yet. Just like all us human doings Peter is more concerned at this stage in his life with discovering where the action is. He's learned that whenever he's around Jesus exciting things happen, and he wants and craves the thrill ride.

Jesus says, "Look Peter. You can't go."

"Aw shucks, come on Jesus. You know I'd go anywhere with you. I'd even die for you," Peter boasted.

The moment turns a bit more serious.

Jesus replies, "No, Peter. You are not ready to do that yet. The point of all this hasn't struck you yet. You missed what I wanted you to really hear because you are still too caught up in the action. Before the rooster even starts waking everyone up tomorrow morning, my accusers will come, and you will say you don't even know me three different times."

At this moment Peter had to have been thinking. What does Jesus know? I'll show him how loyal I am. Of course, I'll be willing to die for him. Just let him wait and see.

***

The heavy footsteps and clanging of the armor could be heard fast approaching their position in the garden. There would be no reason to run this evening. There would be no reason to mysteriously slip away into the crowd as had been done before. This confrontation was necessary. This confrontation was the eternal plan of love coming to its final fruition. Rather than hide or run, Jesus stepped out to face the religious leaders, soldiers, and Judas the betrayer, who had all come to arrest him.

Peter would now have his moment to prove his loyalty. His shining chance to demonstrate to Jesus that he was willing to do whatever it takes to complete the mission. Up until now there had never been any need to violently react to the naysayers of Jesus, but this was a desperate situation. They were not coming to argue or debate this renowned teacher, they were coming to arrest him. Desperate times call for desperate measures.

Peter yanked out the sword he had been so cleverly concealing for just such a time as this. He wasn't going down without a fight. Jesus would see just how loyal he would be. Just how far he would be willing to go. If at first you don't succeed, then take more action! At least that's the motto of a human doing.

The sword sliced through the air, and when it came to make an impact it went right through the ear of the high priest's slave named Malchus. In a do or die, fight for your life situation, who goes for somebodies ear? And who goes for the ear of a slave? Wouldn't you try to take out the biggest soldier by surprise first? Malchus probably wasn't even packing. He probably wasn't allowed to pack. In Peter's big action sequence he not only managed to make an utterly foolish display of his sword wielding ability, but further proved he was missing the bigger point of Jesus' story line. How could slicing off a guys ear possibly jive with the command to love each other?

Peter wanted action. Love and peace were way too boring.

***

So the meditation class had not exactly been up to my speed, but the guy who taught it was a rather intriguing character. He was the Spiritual Life Director of the facility where I was enjoying my twenty-eight day hiatus. A place where the most action one could get caught up in was coloring outside the lines of one of these new trendy coloring books for adults during arts and crafts hour.

The thing I had found most intriguing about him is that we had both shared very similar interest and career paths. In fact, his resume had been pretty action packed. This guy had known how to get things done in life, and now he was the Spiritual Life Director of this boring place. Spending his life with a bunch of knuckleheads like myself. What could possibly have gone so miserably wrong? I had to know. I had to talk with him. My own fate could be weighed in the balance. I made an appointment.

Now I've been doing this pastoring thing for quite some time. As egocentric as I have been in my past, I have always been pretty good at getting you to talk about you. Let's talk about you. Let's not talk about me. I am hiding stuff, so the topic of you is great! One of the things I have learned in recovery is that I've always been very literate when it comes to reading other people's lives, but very illiterate when it came to reading my own. I was headed into this appointment to talk about him. Turns out he was really, really good and somehow—I'm still trying to figure out how he did it—he turned the whole thing around. After a couple minutes of telling me his story, we had somehow ended up on the topic of me.

When I finally caught on that his eyes were glazing over due to my long list of self aggrandized life accomplishments, I decided to admit that I was a bit worried about this boredom thing. What was I going to do in sobriety? I knew I couldn't keep trying to achieve twenty-four hours a day. That made me too tired. But, then when I tried to relax from the action I could never turn my mind off. It was always solving more problems and doing more work. Alcohol was my only way to stop the madness, but it was only causing more madness.

He then looked at me and said, "John, you strike me as the type of guy that is afraid if you find your peace, then you'll lose your edge."

"Wait. What? Say that again."

He said, "Are you afraid that if you find your peace, you will lose your edge?"

Yes! That was exactly it. Somebody had finally put into words what my emotional trauma had been this entire time when I even remotely considered the possibilities of sobriety. I had met these people before. These people with peace. They wore less than professional attire to work, took up odd hobbies like bonsai tree trimming, spent way too much time talking about their feelings, and occasionally even had the audacity to believe one could have a day with nothing planned. These people were obviously crazy and did not understand a capitalistic economy or the capitalistic kingdom. Things must be done. Action must be taken. These people of peace didn't get it.

Oddly enough, I had always been a secret admirer of these people. I had observed them as strange specimens of a foreign origin. I wondered what made them tick, and how they could just sit there. How could they just sit there? I wanted something that I knew they had, but I didn't want to be like them to get it.

The Spiritual Life Director—turns out he was a counselor too—picked up a book by a guy named Dan Harris called "10% Happier" and asked me if I had ever heard of it. Nope. Now I'm notorious for giving away books. I have a few books in my library that I believe everybody should read, so I usually keep multiple copies available so when I'm meeting with someone and the need to read one of these particular books comes up, I can just hand them a copy and say go for it. I thought he was going to give me a copy. Turns out he wasn't. He was also kind enough to inform me that the book was not available in the bookstore, meaning I would have to wait until I left rehab to get my copy. Great! This place was all about teaching you patience.

The day I got out of rehab Tally pulled up and we packed up. My family was waiting for me in Lynchburg, Virginia, about four and a half hours away. On the journey we stopped for some food, and across the parking lot there was a book store. I had been chomping at the bit to get my hands on a copy of this mysterious book. I literally had no idea what it was about, aside from something to do with happiness. This part intrigued me even more and even kind of made me want to read it in order to quickly debunk the whole happiness theory that is so pervasive in today's culture.

Boy, had I ever walked into this one. The book was about meditation. Now I'm not getting into, nor do I care about all the big misconceptions that exist surrounding meditation and what it is or isn't. Just like the concept of prayer plays a part in every major world philosophy or religion, so does the concept of meditation. It's all about what context in which it is chosen to be practiced, but it has largely been ignored by my own faith tradition. My ongoing counselor is a proud self-proclaimed follower of Jesus. He reads his bible everyday in its original Hebrew and Greek expressions. To say the least, he knows a thing or two about ancient scripture. I had become very intrigued at one point as to why I had never been taught the concept of meditation—or in my tradition contemplative prayer—while growing up in American church culture. I told him that I felt people had ignorantly shied away from the concept because of the associations and misrepresentations concerning eastern practice. He wisely looked back at me and said, "John, it's never occurred to any of the detractors that Jesus was an eastern man." Touché!

***

It was my very first morning after rehab, and I was up before the sun. The rest of the house was all asleep. No where to go. Nothing to do. Boring. I walked into my sister-in-law's home office area and had a seat at her desk looking out over the backyard where nature was starting to wake up.

It is pretty crazy to think that you never know when you are going to do that new thing for the very first time that is going to turn into a life-changing habit, whether for better or for worse. Who could have predicted that when I was seventeen years old, down by the riverbank mourning the loss of a high school girl infatuation with the boys, and I popped open that first can of beer, that what I had inadvertently done was open Pandora's box of the worst most destructive force of habit I would ever have to battle? Also, who would have thought that what I was about to do sitting at my sister-in-law's desk would be even more powerful and addictive in the most positive of ways. Don't think that dreaded trip to the gym is just another attempt at health. It may turn out to be the first step to total life transformation.

I had nothing better to do with the morning, so I thought I might go ahead and give this meditation thing a shot. Heck, how could it hurt to breathe and notice it for a few minutes? I still wasn't sure exactly how to do this, so I figured there must be an app that could help me out. We all know there's an app for everything. After a few minutes of searching the various possibilities, I settled in on one, downloaded it, and hit go.

Breathe in. Breathe out. Breathe in. Breathe out.

It wasn't life-changing. It was just breathing and noticing it. It was just being still. It was something I had never done before on purpose. It was the initial stepping into another world that the Creator had placed inside of me. However, it would be months before I would discover the benefits this simple practice was having on my physical and spiritual life. No matter the boredom of that initial moment, I have not missed a day since. It is a chance everyday to just be. It is another step toward Becoming Human.

***

Several weeks after being home and getting back into the regular swing of things a very curious thing occurred. I had been breathing on purpose every morning, and reading everything I could get my hands on about the topic of meditation. Beyond all its spiritual connotations, I was finding all kinds of research that had been done pointing to the fact that there were huge benefits to what it did for ones physical, emotional, and psychological well being. Truth was, I couldn't tell that it was doing anything for me. All I knew was that it couldn't hurt to breathe on purpose and it was supposedly one more tool in my toolbox to battle addiction. So I kept doing it.

I've probably given it away by now, but I can be a rather animated personality. I'm pretty excited about life, and when I'm not excited that can equally express itself in my reactions. I had walked into the kitchen to get something to drink. As

I was opening the refrigerator door there was suddenly a loud crash behind me that occurred at the back sliding glass door. Instinctively, I already knew who the culprit was. My middle son is all out all the time. He earned his nickname of "The Wild Man" before he was even two years old. He works to live up to that monicker on a daily basis, and we love it! However, it does at times have a downside, which can include unexpected sound barrier breaking moments. This was one of those moments. I calmly turned around to asses the situation. Thankfully, the glass door was not shattered, and it did not seem that any crazy injuries had ensued.

I gently said, "Hey bud, try to go a little easier and be a little more careful."

"Yes sir," he replied.

I then began to turn around to continue the process of getting my NON-alcoholic beverage.

Wait. What just happened? That's what went through my head. You too may have noticed a few adverbs in there that don't belong in the description involving the reaction of an animated personality to such a moment—calmly and gently.

Few things I have ever done in life have been done calmly or gently. You know where The Wild Man gets it from. And yet, here I was in this moment feeling as gentle and relaxed as I had before the deafening pandemonium. What was happening to me? If this had been a few months earlier my reaction would have been very different. Upon hearing such a loud crash, a powerful energy would have generated itself from my abdominal core and quickly ascended to the top of my head, where it would have spewed forth out of my mouth and off of my tongue in a way that would have let everyone around me know that the beast within had been awakened in a feeble attempt to mask the fact that the moment had frightened me. That is to say, I would have likely hollered at my son.

In the stuff I had been reading it said that by practicing this thing called breathing, meditation, contemplative prayer, or whatever label you prefer, on a regular basis I could in fact become a calmer, gentler, and even kinder person. A person who felt less stress and more joy. Was it actually happening? Could it be that simply sitting down for a few minutes a day and focusing on my breath was changing me?

The wildest part is that even though I was experiencing a greater level of peace in my life, I was getting more done than ever before. Pastoring, gym, writing, walking, support group meetings, and the early beginnings of a business, were all part of my daily and weekly schedule. The world was benefiting from my productivity, those around me were enjoying my new persona, and I was enjoying a new found friend that I had never known called peace.

So let me ask you. Why not give it a try? Forget all the preconceived notions and misconceptions, and certainly quit worrying that you might look weird doing it. That's just your ego trying to make sure you stay a human doing. Just sit down. Back straight. Close your eyes. Take a big deep breath in. Let it out slower than you took it in. Do that again. Now just breathe normally while focusing on your breath. If a thought comes up, then just let it float away. Just sit there and breathe. Just be. Just be with Him. When you are done, do it again tomorrow, and then the next day and the next. Be patient. Wait to see what happens. It turns out you won't lose your edge when you find your peace.

By the way, that whole thing about sobriety being boring? Hogwash! I've been up since 3:45 AM writing this chapter. There's a whole lot of getting it done in just being.

Love Is Why

People can do some crazy things when they think there is not enough. Black Friday stampedes ensue at the local big box store. Fights can break out over milk and bread at the first hint of snow. Entrepreneurs who have made multi-millions of dollars in a legitimate way, then go down for insider trading. Countries invade other countries for their natural resources. Why do we think we need a little bit more?

This past Christmas we thought my teenage son was going to have a coronary due to his stress level over a particular pair of sneakers that he wanted. This kid has way more shoes sitting on his shelf than I had during my entire childhood. What makes this such a travesty is his foot has not even stopped growing. He will outgrow them all within the year, and there goes that investment. But, here we were at Christmas, and there is this one pair that he just has to have. He has two younger siblings and they weren't even as intense over what they wanted as he was. It began by hinting and then moved into straight up teenage nagging. Everyday we were warned that these kicks were a hot item, and if we were getting them for him, then we had better move now. Without this pair his feet may never know the joy that was available to them. Turns out that we waited too late, and his feet have never known the joy. Don't worry too much about him though, due to our parenting he was already going to have to get extensive counseling as an adult. This just gave him more to talk about in therapy. Plus he's moved on to wanting a different pair already. The point is this whole experience had him acting more like a five year old than thirteen.

What if there's not enough?

This is a question that drives many of us to do what we do, and can be especially crippling for we addicts. It is what makes us act like human doings more than human beings. It is why we so wrongly answer the question that everybody asks us when we are kids, "What do you want to be when you grow up?"

We have come to believe that there are limits to the things that matter in life. That to get our fair share of the things we want, we are going to have to do something for them. We are going to have to earn it. If we are looking for power, then we spend our lives in pursuit of the corner or Oval Office. If we want money, then we ignore time with the kids in order to chase down the next dollar. Should fame be our game, then we work hard at maintaining our less than authentic presence on social media at the expense of our true self. The most dangerous part is that each of these motivating factors—and there are many more—are usually a subconscious desire that was developed from something we felt we were not getting in our childhood. We aren't walking around saying I want power, money, or fame, but underneath the surface we do, and thus we spend our lives human doing in order to achieve those things. All of these internal motivating factors lead us to live lives and chose professions that reinforce our "the stuff we want has limits" viewpoint. This viewpoint leads us to do and pursue more and more, and further and further down the rabbit hole we go.

What internally drives me is the need to achieve or win. There are only so many wins out there, and I found myself in rehab having pursued as many as I could get my hands on. I had been going after the wins of academic success, wins of we scored more points than the other team, wins of getting the girl to marry me, wins of a growing church, and wins of recognition—which was certainly achieved in having to divulge to the whole world that I am an alcoholic—that was tongue in cheek folks. This subconscious need to achieve had allowed me to achieve a lot, but it had also left me wanting more and more. There were not enough wins in life to fill the void. There wasn't enough human doing to ever get what I really wanted. If I was really going to win and achieve enough, then I was going to have to play a different game. It would be a game that would keep score in a much more advanced way, and what I would end up trying to gain would look far different than just winning, and it would not involve more doing.

***

Allow me the freedom to take a sidebar here and say that everybody should go to rehab. Before condemning that statement please allow me to explain. It is not that everybody is living out their addiction in the same self destructive way as I and so many others are. It is to say that everybody has subconscious motivating beliefs and subsequently go-to coping behaviors that are less than beneficial to their own and others' well being.

It is not to say that one should become more self destructive in order to get treatment for it. One of my fellow recovering alcoholic friends likes to say about resentful, unkind, and angry people, "If we could just get them to start drinking, then we could finally get them some help." (Addict humor can be a little on the darker side.)

It is to say that there are things one can learn through the self-awareness process—the process of unpacking those subconscious beliefs—that is offered in treatment that would be beneficial for every human being to know and be able to practice. That's the purpose of this book. If the stuff rehab taught me can alter the life of a self destructive addict, a full blown human doing, then imagine what it can do for the semi-healthy human. This stuff, these simple practices, may just be what catapults you to the next level.

It is to say that if you are self destructive then go get help! Go to treatment. Professionals are there for a reason.

***

That was the free part of the book and was a lead in to mention that the place where I got help was beautiful. I've already described watching the sun rise over the Chesapeake Bay on my first Sunday morning there. During my time I encountered bald eagles and squirrels playing dodge nut, which is their own animalistic version of that dreaded middle school gym class game, dodge ball. One of my favorite spots was under a huge magnolia tree that sits in the middle of campus. Under this tree I could look out over the Chesapeake Bay and stare at the water until everything faded from focus. Actually, it was under this tree that everything else I had been discovering were distractions in life–like trying to win everything all the time–were beginning to fade away.

If my purpose wasn't to achieve, win, or do more, then what was it? What had God intended? Why had God done all of this anyway? Don't tell me you've never thought about it. It's one of the great questions that haunts the human soul. Why are we here? Why do we exist? These are all modified versions of the same longing to know. We fundamentally believe that something as dramatic and dynamic as life should have purpose and meaning. So what is it?

By now you've been able to deduce that my intellectual prowess is not going to drop some mind blowing revelation on you. It's got to stay simple in order for me to run with it. So here's what I've got.

The very first story in this compilation of ancient text called the Bible–to which I have been referring throughout this book–is one in which God sets out to create everything we can see and experience including what is us. We were the last of the masterpiece.

"Then the LORD God formed the man from the dust of the ground. He breathed the breath of life into the man's nostrils, and the man became a living person." (Genesis 2:7)

There's that whole breathe thing again. Seems focusing on it has been important from the start.

Man—ladies please understand that this is short for mankind—was then given a simple set of instructions like be fruitful and multiply, as well as have dominion over all that was created—not a cart blanche pass to plunder and trash it all. On top of this, a special garden was provided for habitation and continued meeting space with God. Sounds non-complicated enough to me. There's not even much required doing involved. So why would God do this then?

The only conclusion that I can possibly draw is that this was about love. How else would love be able to express itself? Love can't be known if there is no one to know it. Love can't be experienced if there is no one to experience it. Love can only be celebrated in relationship. God is love. God brought you and me into existence so that love could have a place to romp, play, and grow.

Now I realize that this is problematic for those of you who have not experienced a whole lot of love in this life thus far. Tragedy, abuse, and less than adequate evident resources can sometimes cloud our ability to tap into the love that so abundantly surrounds us. Many come to wish that God hadn't bothered with love's playground. Many also conclude that since this grand plan seems to have failed due to the pain they have suffered in this life, that God himself must not even exist, and no such love plan is in play. They conclude we are just primordial ooze.

I'm not going to try and debunk all of those doubts and fears in this space. Plenty of greater minds than mine have expounded volumes on this subject. All I've got is an understanding that love can't be a forced thing. The universe is built with laws against that, just like we have laws against relationship by force. Therefore, we have been given a free will. Free to chose love, and free not to. We've all made choices at times to choose it, and we've all made choices at times not to. Those times when we've chosen not to receive love have created a degree of our personal misery and contributed to the collective misery of this planet in its current state. Multiply the freewill choices of "receive or not receive" love of every human who has ever lived, and we are now where we are.

Meanwhile, love is the only thing my feeble mind can come up with in trying to understand the story of our existence. It's what I'm going to go with. It's the only explanation that will keep me sober. If it's weak minded, then so be it. Strong minded landed me in rehab. What better options could there be on this multiple choice "purpose of life" test anyhow?

Why do we exist?

    A.   Love
    B.   Cruel Experiment
    C.   Chance

Love is my choice. It's the most positive of the three, and I need positive. Also, it's not going to hurt anybody if I turn out to be wrong. But, I don't think I'll end up saying, "Oops, I thought love was the answer? My bad."

Under the magnolia tree is when I decided that love would be my best option going forward. It would have to be the new scoreboard I was glancing at to see if I was winning. Love is the true benchmark of a human being, because it is the nature of our Creator.

***

Now you really didn't think that I was going to leave poor Peter back there in the garden looking the fool for having lopped off a guys ear with no chance for further redemption did you?

Well, I probably would, but since that's not how the story actually ends, then I won't.

Continuing with my unofficial interpretation of what they might have said to one another, I'd bet Jesus looked at Peter and said, "Quit playing with the sword already! Peter, it's all fun and games until somebody gets their ear chopped off." Okay, so that's not an exact quote, but you get the idea of Jesus' disappointment with Peter at this moment.

Jesus then made sure that Malchus wasn't going to live the rest of his life with his glasses sitting crooked. Jesus put his ear back on. Jesus was arrested. His disciples dispersed; they were afraid that if they didn't go, then they might be next.

For the rest of the evening Peter involved himself in a high level game of cloak and dagger. He loved Jesus. Jesus had rebuked his sword slashing, ill-fated attempt at freeing him from this moment. Now what was Peter to do?

Peter also loved Peter. He was curious to see what would become of Jesus. What became of Jesus could become of him. He would have to stay close to observe, but not so close that he could be recognized or caught.

Too late! The servant girl walks up, "Hey, you look really familiar to me! Weren't you one of those that was with that Jesus guy who just got arrested?" She was obviously the drama type, and was not asking in order to quietly help Peter out, but rather to bring it to everyone else's attention.

Peter wasn't real quick on his feet. His answer is reminiscent of one of those live cop shows where the less than brilliant criminal mind says to the police officer, "I don't know how that marijuana got in these pants. These aren't my pants!"

Peter says, "Uhhh. Uhhh. I don't know what you're talking about it." With that it was time to find a new place to shrink into the background.

He was a little farther away now. Out by the gate and not so close to the action of Jesus' trial, but still close enough that he could get the latest reports coming out of the ancient courtroom. I am not sure of the vendetta that the servant girls of the region had against Peter. Maybe, he stiffed one of them a tip at some point, but word had obviously traveled fast through their circle, because here comes another servant girl loud and proud with a declaration for all to hear, "This man was with Jesus of Nazareth!"

Peter had thought this one out. He wouldn't be caught again with nothing to say. He got creative with, "I don't even know the man!"

By now the servant girl conspiracy was taking effect on the audience at large. A bit later a few folks who were likely following this court case came over to Peter and said, "Hey. You've got to be one of the guys who was following this Jesus character. You talk just like they do."

Peter had to have been thinking, "Why won't this just go away?" He knew he was going to have to pull out the big guns now.

A life where identity and significance are determined by doing, achieving, and winning is one that must be defended. Not everyone is going to agree with the actions you have taken in order to get to where you are. In order for these actions to have validity, and in turn your identity remain unscathed, you have to fight and defend the actions. Most of us do this with a whatever it takes attitude, even if we have to lie to justify.

My interpretation of Peter's response says, "Hey look! I'm sick of this with you people. I am who I said I am. May I be cursed—which I take it was a pretty big deal in the ancient world—if I'm lying to you!"

I'm imagining that for the rest of his life Peter would remember the sound that he heard next. The sound that would forever remind him of what human doing had done to him. It had caused him to deny the greatest friend he had ever had—three times.

Cock-a-doodle-doo! The rooster crowed.

***

Several dark days had passed since Peter's moment of shame. During this time Jesus had been found guilty of being I AM. In a world of human doings, simple Being is punishable by death. This had sent his followers, including Peter, into hiding.

A few days after the burial of Jesus the ladies came back to the disciples safe house telling them that they had been to the tomb of Jesus earlier that morning, and in spite of their best efforts they weren't able to locate his body. Since when does a body up and go missing? Peter and the boys ran to the tomb to confirm the ladies' findings, because for whatever reason, in every century, we men can't just take the word of the ladies.

Then crazy miraculous stuff starts taking place. Jesus begins to physically show up on several different occasions to the safe house and disciples' meeting space. This is a rather marvelous feat for a dead man. The revelation of his living is designed to spark hope in his team. For some it does, but there is no mention of Peter in this part of the story. That's saying something about Peter, because for a guy who finds himself at the center of attention throughout most of the Jesus plot line, this is an odd time for him not to be saying or doing something. This is not his normal modus operandi.

I'm guessing the couple of times Jesus makes his appearance is when Peter starts to head to the back of the room and slip in behind a few of the other disciples. I'm thinking he may feel pretty ashamed and not much on wanting to chat with Jesus. There is no doubt that he went social media dark.

Although the story doesn't tell us, I am really curious as to exactly how many days are passing here. I'm thinking around 28 days or so. This situation is starting to look to me like Peter has landed himself in rehab. With life as he has known and expected it to be having come crashing down around him, all of his obsessive doing along with needing to be the center of attention having led him to hurt the one he loved most, and now a period of hiding and quiet where he is forced to be taking a hard look at what this whole thing with Jesus was all about anyway? Yep, that sounds a whole lot like rehab to me.

It would seem that soon after these Jesus' sightings Peter concluded that since this whole Jesus story hadn't worked out in the way that he had written it, then he was done. If at first you don't succeed, then go fishing. That's exactly what Peter did.

Fish like to eat breakfast too, and that's why a good fisherman is up at the crack of dawn out on the boat. Peter may not have turned out to be the most skilled swordsman, but he was a good fisherman.

From the shoreline he heard John, one of his disciple buddies hollering, "Peter! Peter! You're not going to believe this! It's Jesus! He's here for breakfast!" Again, my version of the story.

I've never fully understood this next part. It would seem that fishing without your clothes on is how one did it back in the day. Peter puts his robe back on, for which I am sure his fishing friends were eternally grateful, jumps in the water, and made like Michael Phelps in the two hundred meter medley for the shore. It would seem that Peter has decided that running from the one he had denied was no longer the answer. The strategy of forget everything and run had not been soul sufficient. It was now time to face everything and recover.

Breakfast was delicious. Jesus cooked it. That's how I know.

You never get down to business before everybody's bellies are full. But now that breakfast was out of the way, Jesus had a few things he was going to need to take care of with his old pal Peter.

"Hey, Peter. I've got a question for you."

"Sure Jesus. Whatever you want."

I wonder at this point if Peter was so food happy that he didn't see this coming, or if when Jesus started asking the question Peter started writing a story of what this was going to be about and got a big lump in his throat?

"Do you love me?" Jesus asked.

Ouch! That had to have hurt. Jesus cut straight to the chase on this one. He always did. He could have asked, "Peter, after all this time together how could you have said you didn't know me in my greatest time of need? How come you weren't there at the foot of the cross with my mom and John? Why did you desert and abandon me?" Any of those would have been legitimate questions. But Jesus wasn't concerned with the more trivial matters of relationship. He was concerned with the one lesson he knew that Peter had not caught onto that night at supper right before his execution. For Jesus this was all about love. It always had been. It always will be.

"Do you love me?" Jesus asked.

Probably with a bit of a defeated sigh Peter replied, "Yes, Jesus. You know I love you."

"Then take care of my sheep." Jesus responded.

Jesus was not done yet though.

"Peter, Do you love me?"

Peter wasn't always the sharpest tool in the toolbox on these things, but I'm thinking he was beginning to catch on to the significance of this moment.

Humbler than the first time, Peter said, "Yes, Lord, you know I love you."

"Then take care of my sheep." Jesus said again.

When you're broken. When you're down and out. Love will never leave you there. As my pastor says, "Love will win, if you let it." Jesus' final command on the night before his murder had been that he wanted the disciples to love each other the way that he had loved them. Peter had missed that point. Peter had left that evening and three times had blatantly turned his back upon Jesus. He hadn't loved his friend. His friend still loved him though. Jesus wouldn't let Peter go unredeemed in this moment. He wouldn't let him spend the rest of his life on a fishing boat living with the regret of what he had done. Jesus would allow love to undo all the doing that had gotten Peter to this point. Here came the grand finale.

"Peter, do you love me?" Jesus asked.

The full realization certainly hit Peter at this moment because he was visibly disturbed by Jesus asking this valid question for the third time.

Peter responded, "Lord, you know that I love you."

One last time for emphasis Jesus said, "Then feed my sheep."

In that simple command was locked all the meaning of life. It was the thing that Peter had been sent to rehab to discover. Form this point on life for Peter was not supposed to be about doing or achieving. Forget the thrill seeking moments like walking on water and sword fights. Peter had learned to stop doing life and start being love.

***

When my wife came up to visit me for family weekend, we had the opportunity to sit under the magnolia tree together. As we were enjoying the beautiful view and breathing the fresh air, I said to her, "You know it's really crazy. I'm forty-one and I feel like I get to finally decide what I want to be when I grow up. Not what I want to do. That's not really all that important to me anymore. I mean what I want to BE."

One of the most popular and well known books found in the Bible is Revelation. It's the one that speaks of the apocalypse, 666, heaven, and a bunch of other things that are incredibly interesting and at the same time really hard for we mere mortals to understand. I think all the mystery that the book comes cloaked in is what makes it so well known and popular. One of the mysterious versus that catches my attention is Revelation 2:17b.

"To everyone who is victorious I will give some of the manna that has been hidden away in heaven. And I will give to each one a white stone, and on the stone will be engraved a new name that no one understands except the one who receives it."

In most Bibles you will read these words are in red print. This means they are the words of Jesus. I don't have a clue what he's talking about when he's talking about manna—which was heaven bread from an Old Testament story—that's been stored up in heaven. It's probably pretty good though. I am most intrigued by this stone that I'm gonna be given that has my new name on it. I wonder what my name is going to be?

From the moment we are born people start throwing labels on us and expecting things from us. Seconds after our arrival we are declared to be a boy or girl, and some adult lovingly holds us tightly and appoints us with the moniker that we will answer to for the rest of our life. Sometimes someone even looks at us and says, "There's our little President or baseball star." From there on, life becomes a blistering fast paced addition of as many labels and achievements as we can stack up. We move from toddler to kindergartener on to college graduate, from single to married on to three crazies and a dog, from rookie to manager on to owner, and the accolades stack up and we become the very best version of human doing that we can become. But in all the doing do we ever really think about who we are?

For me becoming what I want to BE means shedding all the labels. It's discovering who I was in those moments right after I was born, before anything was assumed or declared about me. It's not about the next public talk I get to give, or the first book that I am privileged to write—this is it by the way. It's not about doing stuff. It's about achieving the essence of presence that God had intended for me when I first became a thought in His infinite mind. When He first planted humankind in a garden to romp and play with love. When my name got written on that stone. It's about trying to discover and fully inhabit the substance of that name. When I enter into the amazing next after this physical life I want to be handed the stone and be able to say, "I knew it! I knew that was my name!"

***

Now before you go dismissing this as far too simplistic or utopian take a moment to really contemplate the implications here. Pay close attention to the implications for your own life. When someone asks you about yourself, does it become a long list of likes and dislikes as well as success and failures? Do you find yourself burnt out and tired in your quest to become? Is life overwhelming? It's likely you misinterpreted that childhood question. It's likely you've been answering what you want to BE when you grow up with a bunch of doing. Sit back and ask yourself the question of what gauges you should really be judging your life by. Should these be trophies or titles, or should we take a look at Jesus final command to love like He loved?

Every night when I lay my head down on the pillow I do a little daily review. It's not like it use to be. I use to go through my day, whether I wanted to or not, and relive every good and not so good moment about it. Writing stories and plotting next steps. I used to fret over how much hadn't gotten done, how much wasn't done the right way, and how much there was still to do. Even as I write this I can see why insomnia was a thing back then. I can see why I felt like I needed a bunch of drinks to get to sleep.

Now it's different. The way I keep score has changed, because I'm playing a different game. It's a game of becoming not of winning. My final thoughts at the end of the day are did I LOVE today? Did I CREATE something today—even if it was just a simple sentence on this page? Did I INSPIRE the people I was privileged to encounter today?

I don't know what that name will be that I will someday discover, but I know its meaning will include those three words: Love, Create, Inspire.

And for me that is now enough.

I'm just curious. If you had three words, what would they BE?

Pay It Forward

The best I can tell is that it had to have been on or around the Friday right before entering into rehab. It was sometime mid-morning or early afternoon, but the particulars would naturally be a bit foggy to me in that I was drunk. Not a kind of fall off the barstool and make a fool of myself kind of drunk, although I have been there, done that, and thrown up on the t-shirt. Rather this was the kind of under the influence that I had come to know as my regular state of affairs. Gone were the days of drinking to feel good and have fun. I was now living the life of full-on addiction where drinking every day at some level was necessary to even just feel normal. This was officially hell on earth, and I was a card-carrying citizen. The worst part was not really even the physical dysfunction that it entailed, although thinking back to that physiological state makes me nauseous even now. The hell entailed was always walking around in a state of fear, resentment, and stress, while utterly alone.

In looking at my life, alone was the last thing that most people would have expected from me. I was a pastor's kid turned Jesus follower at a young age now enjoying the life of an Executive Pastor in a church most would consider fairly big with a beautiful family, great pastor, and wonderful staff. Something tells me that I don't need to explain any further how one could feel alone, fearful, resentful, and stressed out with my background knowing that alcohol was my numero uno relationship. I couldn't be close to anyone else, because that would risk my closer acquaintance with the beloved bottle.

On the afore mentioned day, I was riding in the passenger seat while my wife was driving. Again, due to the fact that I had already been drinking. You wouldn't have wanted someone like me to miss those last few days with the bottle right before I went to rehab? I wanted to make the most of the time I had left. So, here I was in the passenger seat when suddenly my phone, which was connected to the car at the time, began to ring. It was a number I didn't recognize. As a general rule of thumb, I don't answer phone calls from numbers I don't know, but I had been talking to several rehab facilities up until this point and I figured one of them may be getting back to me. My wife got quiet in the background and I answered the phone,

"Hello, this is John."

"Is this John Smith?"

"Yes, it is."

"John, this is Perry Noble."

You may remember this name from the introduction of the book. Perry Noble is a pastor who founded what would become one of America's largest and most influential churches. He is a talented and gifted communicator, and just like myself, he has had his own struggle with alcohol.

Now I have been privileged to both work for and meet some of the most influential folks that God has used in building his kingdom over the course of my lifetime, but it's a pretty big deal in my profession when someone like Perry Noble ends up with your number and uses it. He didn't have to do that, but he did.

During our phone call Perry told me of how he had heard my story through my best friend, Tally, and spent about 10-

15 minutes with me on the phone. He confirmed with me that my church would be finding out about my addiction on that coming Sunday, and told me that it would be rough. He also offered me a great deal of hope by telling me that I would make it through. He shared with me how well he was doing in having come through it, and that God still had great things in store for me. He prayed for me. More importantly he offered me hope in what felt to be a hopeless time.

***

There was another part of this recovery process with which I found myself to be a bit concerned. Don't get me wrong, nothing could have been more concerning than the part where I had to lay my soul bare and divulge all the great and glorious mistakes and hurts that I had caused upon others. This part was not that bad, but at least the amends process would be a relatively brief period in time. The part of recovery that I'm referring to now seemed to have a much longer expected shelf life. The expiration date would be death. This is something that I would have to do from now on. They told me that if I wanted to stay sober that I was going to have to pay it forward. Turns out this is the same thing you have to do in order to stay a human being, and not go back to the doing of that other monster.

The reason this was going to be a problem was that I hate counseling. I know. I know. I am a pastor. You've already determined that something is significantly wrong with me, but did I really have to go into a profession that was going to highlight all of my deficiencies? The answer seems to be yes.

It was my first day of graduate school classes and I was really looking forward to what was to come next. Most of my friends who were headed into ministry were going the traditional seminary route. While I knew that I would eventually want to work in a church setting, I also knew from having grown up in that environment that church life can be volatile at times. This means that crazy stuff happens in churches. Crazy stuff happens to pastors. Turns out that not everybody even likes their pastor. I wanted a financial insurance policy to fall back on in case things did not work out in a more traditional church role. It is for this reason I had decided to get a counseling degree. It made sense. Most of my life folks had told me that I was "wise beyond my years" and that I gave pretty good advice. That's all it takes to be a good counselor, right?

I showed up to that first class primed and ready to go. I don't exactly recall the actual name of the class, but the idea was Counseling 101. My notebook was fresh, my mind was open, and I had no doubt that in no time I would be part of the solution to worldwide pain.

My professor was and still is a fairly well known guy in the Christian counseling ethos. Ironically, what I didn't know at the time, is that he would eventually do the premarital counseling for me and my wife—we had to call in some heavy hitters, but that's another book.

After the initial introductions, making sure we were all in the right class—that nobody was supposed to be in the graduate course for Under Water Basket Weaving being taught next door—he began. What he began with would forever change my view of this all important profession from which I have since so greatly benefited personally.

He began by describing what the day in the life of a counselor was like. This class was an hour long, so I know that his description had to have been much better and more nuanced than what I offer up here, but this is all my brain can muster back from that day.

A counselor comes to the office. A counselor listens to somebodies whining problems. A counselor does paperwork about said persons whining problems. A counselor mind numbingly repeats this process over and over again, until said counselor must seek counseling themselves.

That's what I got out of the class.

Now I have to throw in this caveat. I am fully aware that this is not the existence of a counselor. Some of my closest friends in life are counselors. At one given time in the recovery process I was seeing five different counselors, each contributing greatly to my transformation into becoming human. Counselors are great, wonderful, and everybody should have one. But, not everybody should be one. That includes me, and that's what I discovered on that day.

I think I had the old Bob Newhart skit in mind when I signed up for the class. Its worth the wasted time at work to pull it up on YouTube and watch it with your office mates. It's called "Stop It!"

This lady comes in to see Dr. Switzer (aka Bob Newhart) for a problem that she has been having. The doctor assures her that her problem can be easily rectified and that it will take him no time at all to help her resolve it. She then proceeds to tell him that the problem is she's afraid of being buried alive in a box. A rather common fear I would assume. Not one you spend a lot of time thinking about, but real nonetheless. His simple advice?

"Stop it!"

The skit is hilarious!

That's what I thought counseling was going to be like. Straight forward and to the point, while moving people quickly through the schedule at one hundred and fifty dollars a visit. Not a bad insurance policy, huh?

Having my hopes and dreams dashed by the end of the first class I proceeded to go directly to the registrars office and drop the class. My counseling career had come to an end.

Now here I am all these years later finding myself in recovery being told that I had to take what I learned and share it with other addicts. That was sounding a whole lot like counseling to me. I wasn't exactly excited about the prospects. Paying it forward didn't sound all that fun. My attitude toward the whole concept kind of reminds me of another Jesus story. This time he is the one telling it.

***

The story can be read in the New Testament book of Matthew and it brings an ominous warning to those who have been given much or have received grace and choose not to pay it forward with their own generosity. It's not a true story, or at least Jesus never claimed it to be. It was one of the many that he told that fall into the category of parable. The kind of story that he told to make a point.

Now I am gonna do what I have done this whole time when relaying one of these Bible stories to you. I'm gonna give it to you the way I read it, and if you want the original you can go look it up yourself. This one is in Matthew 18:21-35.

There was this king whose coffers seemed to be running a bit short on cash. There was this new pair of Air Jordan's that were dropping on Tuesday, and so he decided to call in some debt so he could grab them up before they were gone.

Okay, none of that last part is true, so I'll try to stick a little closer to the actual story line. Just wanted to see if you were paying attention to what you are reading.

The king really did want to call in some debt, so he started with the guy that owed him millions. That's who I would have started with too.

This guy was not good for the debt that he owed, so the king figured the fastest approach to debt recovery would be to just go ahead and sell the guy into slavery along with his wife and kids. He would take that money, while also selling everything else the guy had in life, and then they could call it square. This king was no joke. He made annoying debt agencies seem like something for which to be thankful.

I guess the guy did the only thing you can do if you are thrust into this kind of situation. He got down on his hands and knees and graveled. He cried like a baby and pleaded for an extension to his debt due date. He promised that he would payback every dime he owed the king, if he would just give him a little more time.

The king suddenly had a moment of mercy rush over him. Rather than just extend the due date, he decided to completely forgive this guy of his millions in debt. If only your credit card company would do this for your charges in the month of December, right?

The guy left the king's presence. This was a brand new start! He did not owe any money. This meant any money that people owed him would go straight into his personal bank account. He would not have to be just turning around and writing a check back to the king anymore. There might be a chance to get ahead, if he could just get the people that owed him to ante up.

He took off to find a fellow servant that owed him a few thousand dollars. He went mafioso on him quick, jerked him up by the neck, and demanded payment. This fellow servant of the king couldn't pay. He too begged and pleaded for an extension, but this previously forgiven debtor was having none of it. The forgiven debtor immediately called in law enforcement and had this guy that owed him arrested.

A few of the guys that were standing around and watching all this go down couldn't believe what they were seeing. They probably knew the king had been gracious to this jerk, and now he's breaking bad on one of their buddies. They took the whole story straight to the king.

The king called the forgiven debtor back in for another meeting, and had a few choice words for the one he had previously shown so much mercy upon. The way the king saw it, since he had forgiven this guy of millions, then maybe the guy should have been willing to forgo a few thousand by offering forgiveness to his fellow man.

The king threw this guy into prison and back into the king's debt.

It would seem that Jesus' point to the story was a reinforcement of his earlier teachings that to whom much is given much is also expected, as well as the human beings responsibility, summarized by Peter's experience, to love.

***

In spite of this ominous warning of Jesus, and assurances that this would be the only way to keep from turning back into Mr. Hyde, I still had my doubts about paying it forward. You see giving stuff away has never really been my thing. It pains me to admit that.

It's hard to recall when I became so stingy. My earliest recollection of innate stinginess had to be around the age of six or seven. I had a friend from school named Aaron. From what little I can recollect, Aaron and his family didn't have a lot of resources available to them to begin with, and that was before the fire.

At some point along the way I had invited Aaron to come to the church that my dad was pastoring at the time. That invitation sounded something like, "Hey, Aaron. You should come to my church sometime. We could play there too, just like here at school." Aaron's response was, "Awesome! I'll ask my mom and dad."

This invitation included zero information on what the church's name was, where it was located, or how to get there. It was a simple invitation from kindergartener to kindergartner. Our parents never spoke about it. One Sunday morning soon after, Aaron and his whole family showed up at our church building for services. They had climbed in the car and took off to find the church of this friend of Aaron's from school. This was long before Google or Waze. They drove past several churches. They pulled randomly—if you believe in that kind of thing—into the parking lot of the church to which they had been invited. They liked it. They kept coming and became a part of our faith community. Then it happened.

One Sunday morning my mom sat me down on the floor of my room and said she had something that she had to tell me. She proceeded to inform me that Aaron wasn't going to be at church that morning because the night before his house had burned down. Everybody in his family was okay, but they had lost everything they owned. This was the first time that anything like this had ever happened to anyone I knew. I asked my mom what Aaron and his family were going to do? She explained that we as a church would be helping them out, but that meant each of us was going to need to chip in and do what we could personally do to help them recover. In my mind this meant that I was off the hook. I was a kid. How could I possibly do anything in this situation? I didn't have any resources that would be any good. My mom then mentioned my Hot Wheels collection.

Some of my earliest childhood memories are of being in the floor playing Hot Wheels with my dad. Dad has always been a big lover of cars and so I think my collection may have been more for him than they were for me. If you have kids you know how this works. However, I loved my collection too. It was the perfect toy, because they were cheap—good for a family on a 1980's small church pastor's salary—and durable. I had quite a few, because if I was good on our Sunday evening grocery store excursions I would get to pick one out. Believe it or not, I was actually good every once in awhile.

I played with these cars all the time. From the bathtub to the yard, they had jumped, raced, swam, and flown through every type of imaginative adventure my little mind could conjure. My mom was now mentioning that I should give some of them up. Maybe Aaron would like a few? All of his were gone.

This wasn't the absolute worst idea I had ever heard. I really did like Aaron a lot, and hated that this had happened to him. I knew I would be sad if it had happened to me and I had lost all my toys. I figured I could spare a few for this cause, and so I told my mom she could count me in.

I went to my room and pulled out the metal lunchbox of The Fall Guy—I'm disappointed that show hasn't ever made it's way to Netflix—in which I kept the cars, and dumped them out on the floor. I then begin to pick out what I felt were quite a few cars, enough to give my friend a decent start to what would be his new collection. I proudly carried my little arms full of cars into my mom and said, "Here mom! I picked out some cars to give Aaron."

Mom was very gracious with what happened next. There was not even an air of disappointment in her expression or tone. This was simply a teaching moment, and I was going to get the chance to learn.

The amount of cars that I was willing to give Aaron turned out not to be an issue. The condition of the cars I had chosen on the other hand was a matter of loving discussion. First of all, I am a brand name snob. I know this has much to do with my ego again. Over time folks knew that I liked toy cars and so I would get them as gifts or special prizes. Many times this meant that they weren't actual Hot Wheels. They were often cheaper knock offs, and in some cases even plastic, not cast iron. Can you hear the disdain in my head even now? Also, I had some cars that had been through more of my imagination than they could handle, and they weren't exactly road worthy anymore. Aaron had a need. I had the chance to meet Aaron's need by meeting my need to keep my toy car collection at a premium quality. This was perfect! I gave him what I didn't want anymore.

I can't quote mom on precisely what she said, but it was something about what would you want somebody to do for you, giving your best, and how good you can feel when you are generous. What happened next is still a bit of a blur. Mom didn't make me—or even guilt me for that matter—but somehow I went back to my room and mustered the generosity to pick out some of my favorite cars and give them to Aaron. I don't recall doing that part, but I know it happened because I remembered in the weeks to come that whenever I was at Aaron's new house playing with his cars, I was secretly wishing they were still mine. Giving stuff away has never really been my thing.

I guess that is a reality for most of us human doings. We do so much because we want so much. When we get what we think we want, then we don't want to give any of it away because we think there is a limited supply of it. That's not the case with a thing called love. Turns out that the only way you get to keep being love is by continuing to dish it out.

***

There's a guy named Bill that I have learned a whole lot about over the course of the past few years. In many ways his story has become the stuff of legend. His life's work has impacted millions of people worldwide. Books and documentaries galore abound about his life and experience. Despite all of this he is only really well known in a particular circle of people. Turns out it's my circle of people, alcoholics.

Bill Wilson is the founder of Alcoholics Anonymous. A group of self-proclaimed recovering drunks that get together as often as necessary to share stories of inspiration and hope.

There is a story that I heard about Bill along the way, and I don't really know if it's legend or true, but it's good, so I'm running with it.

After years of hard and destructive drinking Bill had just recently climbed up on the wagon—that's alcoholic jargon to say that he had quit boozing it up. He was really getting a lot out of his new sober way of life, and he couldn't help but think of all his old drinking buddies who were still living it up in their anger, fear, and resentments. He decided that he wanted to do something about that so he began taking his message of hope to as many of them as might give him an ear. It turns out that addicts are hard core human doings. They like what they do and they want to keep doing it. Bill was having little to no success and he was beginning to get depressed because of it.

One day Bill went home in a despondent mood and expressed his discouragement to his wife. He told her of all the efforts that he had been making and how it seemed that no one even cared to listen, or if they did, it was only for a brief time and then they were out drinking again. No one had stayed sober for any length of time as a result of his work.

His wife was a very wise woman. She looked at him and said, "Bill, how long has it been since you have had a drink?" Bill responded, "Well, you know. It's been months now." She said, "Then all your efforts have worked for one person, you."

***

So this is why a guy like Perry Noble would give me a call. He was paying it forward. He was actively engaged in the process of becoming human. His time on the phone with me hadn't been a counseling session. It had been an empathetic "I've been there, done that" statement of solidarity. He was paying it forward.

When we as human doings fail and make mistakes other human doings run around and say things like, "Look what they did! I'm glad I haven't done that." Human beings aren't quite like that though. You know a human being because they are the ones that are not focused in on the deed, but rather on the doer. Human beings say things like, "Wow, I've done the same thing, let me help you out." Or, as another of my recovering friends likes to say, "I'm glad I haven't done that, yet." A human being knows there is always a possibility of a "yet" given the right amount of time and circumstance. A human being knows they too could find themself in the same heap of challenge as their fellow servant.

Perry didn't know me and he certainly couldn't have picked me out of a line up—I've never been in a line up, yet. But he had been down a similar road I was traveling. I don't know how his story played out in early recovery, but somewhere along the way he had to have experienced some extraordinary forgiveness and love, because on this day he had plenty to give away to me. That's the secret of those who have been forgiven and loved. They know that there is plenty more where their's came from. They know they could give away their entire Hot Wheels collection and more would eventually show up somehow. They know that forgiving thousands of dollars of debt would beget millions of dollars worth of joy. They know the peace of pulling over in the storm to help a fellow traveler find safety.

A little over a year after that phone call I had the chance to send Perry a thank you email. The following is a slightly edited excerpt of that interaction.

"I have wanted to thank you personally not only for that call of a lifetime, but also because without your story mine could have looked very different. You see the best I can tell, a year before my own debacle, Tally sent me a text one Sunday afternoon. It was the announcement concerning your own struggle and subsequent departure from your church. Tally did not know he had sent that text message to an alcoholic. As I read about what was probably one of the worst days of your life, I was overwhelmed with the feeling that I would soon follow a similar storyline if I did not get help. That afternoon I called my best friend and got honest about my struggle for the first time, with someone other than my wife. This set off a beginning for me in which I tell folks that I dipped my toes in the waters of recovery. I began seeing a counselor, attending a few support meetings, got honest with my pastor, and curtailed a bit of my drinking. It didn't take. I would still have to be drunkenly pushed into lake recovery, and learn to swim, but I am ever so grateful that your own courage and story inched me close enough to the waters for me to stumble headlong into my new life."

His reply was ever gracious. It was the reply of a human being.

***

The truth is it's grown on me by now. This whole idea of paying it forward. It doesn't feel like counseling to talk with someone in the midst of transformation from human doing into human being. I certainly don't just tell them to stop it. I'm over my Hot Wheels grief. In fact, if I can ever find that

Fall Guy lunch box in the attic, I'm going to give the rest of the collection away.

Stingy can still be a struggle, but having experienced love I've come to recognize that it won't be running out anytime soon. Actually, it'll keep growing as long as I keep paying it forward.

The First Thought: Thankfulness

'm a T.V. sleeper. If you are one, or you live with one, then you already know what I'm talking about. If you live with one, then I have just provided one more reason for you to dislike me.

We T.V. sleepers need noise. It's another sign of our human doingness. The noise from the television gives us something to concentrate on in order to slow down our minds from racing to a thousand other places which would otherwise keep us awake until the wee hours of the morning. How people managed to do this sleep thing in the stone age is beyond me.

It was before the crack of dawn, and I knew that it would be a few hours before Tally woke up. We were headed on a ministry trip to Knoxville, Tennessee, but had a day to kill so we stopped over into my old stomping grounds in Newport, Tennessee. There is a bunch of my dad's side of the family that live there—practically everybody in the county—and I had called it home from my seventh grade year through high school graduation. Since I knew I had a few hours to kill, I quietly slipped out of the hotel room, grabbed the rental car, and went cruising down and around memory lane.

A couple of hours passed and when I arrived back to the hotel room I was not prepared for what I was about to witness. As I walked into the room, Tally was sitting on the edge of the bed trying to get his shoes on. You could tell that he had already showered and dressed, but he did not look good at all. He looked like he had been hit by the proverbial freight train, and I thought he was sick. I think the conversation went something like:

"Hey, man. You okay?" I said.

"No, I'm not!"

This was his gracious and ever so kind tone. You know. The kind that only old friends can share in a moment like this.

"What is wrong? Are you sick?" I inquired.

"No, I'm not! I didn't get any sleep last night."

And he said it like it was my fault, but I wasn't quite catching on.

"Yeah, I thought the bed was a bit hard myself," with an empathetic bent in my voice.

"It wasn't the bed! It's the fact that I was in the middle of the Vietnam War all night!"

"What are you talking about?" I asked.

This one had me really curious. I was thinking there was the possibility of a psychotic break happening to my friend.

"That stupid T.V. that you have to sleep with on the History Channel! All night the shows are about war. There was constant gunfire and explosions. I was tossing and turning with the worst dreams. How can you do that to yourself every night? I am never sharing a hotel room with you again!"

War as background noise for dreamscape probably was not the best for a guy like Tally who grew up in the most challenging neighborhoods of East Baltimore, but maybe he had a greater point to which I needed to be paying attention. What was I doing to myself every night?

***

By this time in the progression of my disease, every night looked essentially the same. Go home and unwind with a drink, then another, then another. Eventually, I would have enough that by sometime around eleven to midnight I would drift off to dream on the couch. Most nights I was ashamed to sleep in my own bed, because I didn't want my wife to have to smell the alcohol seeping through my pores and coming off my breath. Needless to say, when I fell asleep the living room T.V. was still on.

Somewhere around two to four o'clock in the morning the alcohol would start to wear off, and I would awake with the next round of insomnia waiting to ensue. The only remedy was to get up, go to the fridge, grab a couple more beers, and hopefully drink my way back into an oblivion. If all this is sounding really horrific, and you are wondering if it's necessary to even share, then know I only share in order to relate to you that addiction is its own version of hell on earth, and it's real! If we don't become human beings, then our human doings will kill us.

I left the T.V. on in order to go back to sleep, because the alcohol alone wasn't enough to turn off my racing mind. My choice of early morning television was of the most uplifting and inspirational nature. Tongue in cheek again folks. Typically, it was a rerun about a serial killer, war, or other crimes against humanity. This was a fantastic combination for a sleeping mind. Alcohol, along with death and destruction, equals a very vibrant dream life. I would do this to myself every night and then be perplexed as to why I was having so many bad dreams and how my days were filled with fear, resentment, and stress.

Now before judging me too hard with thoughts like, "Well, of course you were a wreck in the mornings with that kind of catastrophic nocturnal behavior." Take a moment to discern that each of us have built up habitual patterns in our human doingness that are impacting our days and shaping our futures. Often these are patterns we can't see ourselves, and it takes something or someone to come along and jar our reality enough to help us discover just what kind of numbskulls we are doing instead of humans we are being.

It wasn't until someone in rehab said something about my "first thought" that it would all click as to how and why this pattern wasn't working and what about it would need to change.

Yes, I said someone said something. That's about as solid of a citation as I can provide for this particular lesson in becoming human. Sometimes the best lessons come from out of nowhere. Guess that's why we are supposed to stay open and ready to learn at all times.

***

My roommate in the early days of rehab was a very interesting character. We didn't have much in common except an adoration for the substance called alcohol, but we got along great. If finding a down to earth, laid back, clean and organized roomie in a college dorm can be difficult, then it would certainly seem impossible in a place like this. God knew I needed no extra drama in my life at this point. Thankfully, he spared me the theatrics. He gave me a good roommate.

There was one little quirky thing that my roommate would do when the annoying attendant would hammer our door with his fist at six in the morning and scream, "It's time to get up!" My roommate would then come alive with a string of expletives often put together in very creative ways. I couldn't help but laugh at the interesting way that he seemed to enter the land of the living each morning.

I didn't think much of his early morning rants of profanity until someone in some class at rehab said something about your "first thought". The best I can recall was that the question was proposed, "What is your first thought of the day?" This is something that I had never given any consideration.

***

What was my first thought of the day? How did it impact the way I got out of bed, or at this time, off of the couch in the morning?

The person teaching us this first thought concept seemed to believe that the first thought of the addict or human doing would typically be about themselves. I decided to put this theory to the test and start seeing if I could record and pay attention to my day's first thought.

This did make me ask my roommate about his first thoughts of the day. I knew what they were because he hollered them out loud, but I asked him what was so bad about coming into the day that caused him to cuss it out first thing? With a big laugh he said, "Wow! I didn't even know I did that." Guess I wasn't the only one that wasn't paying attention to my first thought.

***

The experiment played out for multiple mornings and I soon discovered the thesis of the first thoughts teacher to be true. I did think of myself first. The worst part was that it was usually something negative. Some crazy judgement that I was casting down upon myself for waking up in rehab, or some thought of a possible negative consequence that I would have to face when I got out. These thoughts would set off an immediate chemical reaction in my body that would result in the usual feelings of fear, resentment, or stress. I was off to the negative races before my feet even hit the floor.

You don't have to be the sharpest tool in the shed to begin to conclude that poor sleeping patterns, alcohol, and stories of mayhem playing in the background while you are unconscious also play a part in what that first thought is going to be. We have all had that experience of the bad dream right before waking which carries itself over into how we treat the dog in the morning, or everybody else throughout our day.

So now that some awareness to my first thoughts problem had come to light, the question became how was I going to change my first thought in the morning from the selfish negativity of a human doing into the life altering thankfulness of a human being?

***

Mary and Martha were sisters way back in the day. Apparently alliterating your children's names is a time honored tradition. Like many siblings these two were polar opposites in their approach to life.

One day they got wind that their friend Jesus was coming to town, so they decided to invite him over to the house for dinner. We have all been caught up in the last minute preparations of unexpected dinner guests. Piles of laundry must get hidden under the bed, unsorted mail gets even more unsorted and thrown in any drawer where space can be found, and the carpet gets vacuumed for the first time since the last unexpected guest came over. Please tell me this isn't just my life? Imagine the challenge since it was Jesus coming over. That would mean that things could not just be moved around and hidden. He's Jesus. He may not have had x-ray vision, but he had other ways. Be sure your hidden mess will find you out!

Jesus arrived with his disciples in tow, and the story told in Luke 10:38-42 seems to imply that there were a few other guests there too. If you are going to have the Savior of the world over for dinner, it would only make sense to make the most of it with the folks in the neighborhood. Once Jesus was there Mary made sure to get the best spot for the show which was sitting at this great storyteller's feet. She didn't want to miss a piece of the action. Dinner wasn't quite finished, but from everything Martha could observe it seemed Mary was.

Martha was rushing around in the kitchen and making things happen. Everything had to be just right. These ladies weren't independently wealthy. That meant they could not hire anyone to do the ice sculpture of Noah's Ark, and getting all the details of each animal carved with precision was a mind boggling task. It was up to Martha alone now. She had lost Mary to Jesus.

Every time Martha glanced at her "To Do" list her human doing became a little more overwhelmed. Overwhelmed is nothing more than a sneaky form of anxiety couched in a false belief that if we can just do enough, then we and everybody around us will be happy. As Martha's anxiety grew, so did her animosity toward Mary. How could Mary just sit out there at the feet of Jesus and act as if there was nothing else to be done? Why would she be so selfish as to abandon her to all the dinner work while she just hung out with the special guest? Martha was angry. This was typical Mary stuff. Mary was always the one caught in the moment, and missing the bigger picture that there were things to be done in life. It's not always about hanging out and having a good time, or so was Martha's take on the situation.

I'm willing to take a bet here that Martha had trouble going to sleep at night too, and that her first thought in the morning was self-centered. Had Ambien been available back in the day I'm sure she would have had a recurring monthly subscription at her local pharmacy. She was all kinds of a hot mess, and while she resented Mary, it was what Mary had that she most needed a dose of. Jesus knew it.

Martha having had all of her sister's laissez-faire attitude that she could handle, she finally decided to use Jesus in order to set Mary straight. This is what folks who are focused on doing, do. They use remarkable Beings like Jesus to try and control the doings of others. This is how religion is birthed. The perversion of being turned into doing.

Martha throws down her apron in disgust and decides to finally confront Mary's laziness head on. She boldly walks into the living room to engage Jesus in her ego's conflated demand for personal justice.

She asks, "Jesus, don't you think that it's completely unfair that I am the one in the kitchen doing all the work while Mary just sits there at your feet getting to enjoy your stories and hob nob with the neighborhood? It would be great if you would tell her how selfish she is being and that she should get her butt up and into the kitchen to give me a hand."

Of course, Jesus was going to be able to see the great injustice that was being propagated by Mary and demand better of her now that Martha had been so kind as to bring it to his attention, right? No, Jesus always saw right through a human doing.

He replied, "Martha, relax. Take a deep breath. Why are you so strung out by all these details? Nobody needs an ice sculpture. Mary's being exactly who she's is supposed to be. She knows what is important, and that's not getting a bunch of stuff done. It's being here with me and the others. She's grateful for the relationships in her life and the love that she experiences because of me. I'm not going to ask her to become ungrateful, task driven, and change anything. I think maybe you could learn from Mary's playbook on life."

That's what every sibling wants to hear. Be more like your sister. Ouch!

Jesus' words were a clear call to Martha to sit down and be thankful to just be.

***

It was time for me to take a play out of Mary's life myself. It was time to try and alter that first thought of the day from being one of negative selfishness to one of positive thankfulness. I really had my doubts though as to whether this could even work. You see I had attempted this once before and the thankfulness strategy had seemed to be a colossal failure.

It was the very beginnings of my active addiction cycle, nine years earlier. My wife and I had just moved with our young son across the country in order to launch a new life. The reality was that it had been a decision that I had made with an addictive mindset. An emotionally based and pain avoiding decision that only ended up causing more pain.

The greatest pain that we were beginning to feel as the result of this decision was that of financial struggle. Up until this point in life we had always enjoyed way more than most families our age. We had both entered marriage as already established working professionals. Poor days of peanut butter and jelly sandwiches had never been our newly wed experience. We had been able to buy a house, place a substantial amount into savings, and eat at nice restaurants. For a guy who had grown up seeing the economic woes of ministry life, I was proud to be proving that it could be done a different way. Life was economically good. One emotional move and it all began to fall apart.

It doesn't take long at all for savings to disappear when there are fewer zeroes showing up on the paychecks. My pride was dissipating with every trip I made carrying hot water from the stove in order to heat the bath tub for my little boy to be able to have a warm bath. Our hot water heater was run off of the oil tank out back, and we couldn't afford to buy the oil for it. We had gone from nice restaurants to Hamburger Helper. My human doing need to be provider was being crushed by the hard realities that life was not always fair.

This early leader of the church named Paul, who wrote a bunch of letters that have been compiled in the New Testament, once said, "Be thankful in all circumstances." Without any other strategy to run with, short of robbing a bank in order to end my financial woes, I thought why not give thankfulness a shot. The problem was that I was about to treat thankfulness the way that Martha treated dinner with Jesus. It was just another thing to do, and not a way to live.

Having mapped out what I believed to be the best strategy for thankfulness success, I sat down with my wife one evening and laid out the plan. I had two dry erase markers in two different colors. There was one for her and one for me. I explained that we would use the markers to write on our bathroom mirror every morning. We would write the top three things that we were thankful for on that day. By doing this first thing in the morning I was hoping that it would at least get my attention pointed in the right direction, and off of the impending doom story that I was so masterfully crafting.

Day one seemed to go well. While I don't recall exactly what I wrote it was something to the effect of wife, son, and roof over our heads—for now. Day two expanded into being thankful for my mom, dad, and sister. Day three was church, transportation, and Hamburger Helper. I can't recall anything that my wife had written, but I can recall something that she hadn't written enough for my ego's sake. I thought that I would be at the top of her list everyday, but as it turns out I was not. So much for being the center of the universe. Day four was—well it was at this point in the week that I started to run out of stuff for which I thought I could be thankful. It was around day four where project thankfulness was terminated. From this point I would continue my decent into full blown active addiction.

So you might be able to see why I was so hesitant to take up yet another thankfulness project at the beginning of my real recovery. I had already predetermined that such a strategy could not work based off of previous experience. However, I knew that if I wanted to continue the recovery from a human doing toward becoming a human being, then I had to figure out a way to alter the day's first thought. Thankfulness seemed to be the best path, but why had my strategy failed while Mary's had been such a success?

Mary was in the moment with Jesus. The only thing that was going on in her life were the things that were going on in her life in that instant. Anxiety over how the meal was going to turn out was not necessary because that was the future. Depression over the actions of her past were not necessary because those were old news, and obviously Jesus didn't care, because he had still come to have dinner with her and given her one of the best seats in the house. Mary wasn't focused in on the past or future of life, she was present. She could only see the here and now. It was in the moment where she saw the things for which she was thankful.

***

That gave me an idea. Maybe I had failed the first time around because I was focused on the broad strokes of thankfulness. It is just like a human doing to only see the big happenings of life, and ignore its finer details. Sure family, friends, and basic provisions are something to be thankful for, but to only see those things is to miss the small brushstrokes of grace that are outlining and accentuating the human being within you.

I had already tried to alter my first thought, by just saying, "When I wake up in the morning, I'm gonna think about something for which I am grateful first." No matter how hard I tried to will this to be, I would still find myself thinking selfishly or negatively in those first few moments of morning consciousness. Most of the time I was in the bathroom before it would dawn on me that I was supposed to be thinking positively and non-selfishly about my day. Since the pull toward a selfish and negative first thought was so strong within me, I knew that I was going to need a simple practice that could rewire my brain toward morning positivity.

***

There are a plethora of journals scattered about my house. One of the reasons is that in many ways I am still old school. I like reading a real newspaper where your fingertips get all inky. There's something exhilarating about taking the risk of a paper cut while turning the page on a real book, and nothing helps me channel my inner Ernest Hemingway more than a cool journal. I have no idea how he actually wrote a rough draft, but if it wasn't the way I imagine it, then please don't ruin it for me. In my mind he used really cool, worn out looking journals.

The second reason is that I rush out and buy a new journal every time I have a grand new writing idea. You gotta wonder why this is my first book, if I have so many journals, but you would know if you were to randomly walk around my house and pick one up. There isn't anything in them. Every journal that I have can be read in the space of about thirty seconds, because no more than the first page or three have any writing in them. The grand idea gets started and then quickly forgotten about or brushed aside. I write just enough that the journal can never be used for any other purpose. Just enough so that when the next grand idea comes about I have to go out and buy another journal. However, there is one journal that is close to full, and I'm already looking forward to its sequel. It is my gratitude journal. It is tracking my growth as a human being.

***

There would be no writing on the bathroom mirror this time. It was too much work erasing one day to put the next day up. Anyhow, if I did this right, then I would want a more permanent record of what I had written day to day. Journaling was the way to go. I bought my new journal and then set the rules for its use.

Every evening before bed time I would sit down and write a few things I was thankful for that same day. Unlike the failed attempts before, I would work on making these much more specific to what had been occurring in my life on that particular day. No more broad strokes. I would now be focusing in on the detailed nuances that only one who is taking the time to be a human being would notice. For instance, here are couple of my journal entires:

May 16
*More words written for first book
*Continued revelations of God my Father and reality
*Dinner around family table

May 17
*One Year of Recovery!

June 18
*Hard days that create the opportunity for practice
*Good friends to have conversation with

The big plan was that having written a few things for which I was thankful the night before, I would then place the journal on my night stand beside my bed. When I awoke in the morning I would try not to think any thought before I grabbed the journal and read one of the items from the previous day. In this way my first thought would center on thankfulness and not selfishness. Oh well, that plan didn't work either.

The moment I awoke the next morning I opened my eyes and turned immediately toward my nightstand. As my hand reached out to grab the journal it happened. I experienced the first thought of the day. I had not been able to get to the journal quick enough. Thinking had beat me to the punch again. But wait. This thought was different from most mornings' first thoughts. In fact, it sounded rather familiar in my head almost like I had rehearsed it or something. My thought was that I was thankful for this journal, and for this new practice of gratitude that I had decided to try out. It was official. My first thought of the day had turned grateful! Although I had already won on day one, I decided to go ahead and play along and finish this simple practice. I opened the journal and wrote my first thankful entry:

September 6
*The beginning of this journal

That was the last morning that I had to practice my first morning thought using the journal. Yes, I continue to write what I am thankful for on a daily basis, but I don't have to use it to prompt my first morning thought. Turns out that practicing thankfulness on life's micro level throughout the day leads to healthier sleep patterns and morning thoughts that invigorate you for whatever challenges your being may encounter for that day. It's a way better practice than nightly mayhem and madness. Who knew?

I Am A Grateful…

Here's where things start to get a little controversial. I've watched people grimace when I say this. There have been people that just slightly turn their head in that "your statement is interesting and I'm not sure what to make of it" type of way. There are those who have looked at me as if I am some sort of heretic to my faith. How dare I make such a statement! Then there are those who want to believe it is true for me, because if such a radical statement could be true for me, then it might mean that the same is true for them. Maybe what is broken in them, as a result of so much human doing, can be repaired. Maybe they too can become human beings, if the statement is true. Maybe they can turn their greatest moment of defeat into their greatest victory. Just for the record, I can't claim a copyright on the statement I'm about to make. I learned it from listening to a few others say it along the way. I too was confused when I first heard it, and then stunned when I realized what the folks saying it really meant.

As a recovering alcoholic I go to these meetings with other people who have my same predilection toward drink. There are people in these meetings that are at every level of transformation from human doings into human beings. There are folks that show up and you can still smell beer on their breath, and there are others that have enjoyed sobriety for more decades than I have been alive. Everybody is welcome. All you have to have is a desire to quit drinking. With that you are in the club.

In these meetings people share stories about how they are overcoming their addiction, or how they have recently slipped up and are trying again. Before you share whatever is on your mind it's polite to mention your name to the group and your human doing or bad habit of choice that gave you the ticket of admission to the meeting. Most people keep this pretty basic with something like, "My name is John, and I'm an alcoholic." And there are always a few creative souls that find a way to spice the intro up a bit. There is one intro that is used more often by those who have been attending these meetings for awhile. These folks are often considered the old-timers—which is a term of respect among the group. It means they have done the hard work of overcoming their addiction, and have discovered the mysterious realms of what it means to be a human being. When these folks speak, you listen. Even if it's just their introduction.

"Hello, my name is—insert the name of the wisest person you know—and I'm a grateful and recovering—insert their place of brokenness or human doing here."

If I am saying it, it sounds like,

"Hello, my name is John and I am a grateful and recovering alcoholic."

You may be asking what's so controversial about that? Wouldn't anybody who has struggled with such a life threatening condition as addiction to alcohol be grateful that they are recovering? That's a simple, "Yes." But, there's more to that statement.

The statement doesn't say, "I am grateful TO BE a recovering alcoholic." Recovery is only one part of it. It says, "I am a grateful AND recovering alcoholic." Or, "I am a grateful alcoholic. I am a recovering alcoholic." There is an attitude of gratefulness for the alcoholism itself, and as you can see that is where the controversy arises.

If you find yourself grimacing, I understand. I did too a bit, at first. How could someone be grateful for actually being an alcoholic? As I have conveyed in a censored, made for T.V. audience kinda way throughout this book, addiction is its own version of hell on earth. Fear, resentment, and stress are the name of the daily game all leading to utter aloneness, and that's just for the person who is addicted. What about all the people who have to spend life in the general vicinity of the addict, because that addict is their spouse, mom or dad, co-worker, or the innocent victim of the addict's intoxicated operation of a vehicle. What could there possibly be to be grateful for in all of that?

***

Hopefully, through the stories I have shared you've come to see that the Bible is not a book of religiously perfect people. I am not exactly sure how it has garnered that reputation except that the "know it all's" and "I'm better than you" folks have misrepresented it to declare their own self-righteousness. A simple reading of any of its stories quickly reveals that it is a compilation of stories about broken human doings who encounter the love of God and either chose to ignore it or receive it. This decision determines whether they will stay a human doing or become a human being. Joseph is just one more of these characters.

Joseph's story can be found in the very first book of the Bible, Genesis chapters 37-50. It is an extensive, but worthwhile read. I will just give you some of the highlights.

Joseph is born into a rather well-to-do and big family. He was the youngest of the bunch, and often times being the youngest comes with special privileges. In this case, Jacob, his dad, publicly declared that Joseph was his favorite, and gave him a special fancy, flashy and colorful coat to wear in which he could strut his stuff. Joseph made the most of the opportunity. His brothers hated him for it. Funny how we human doings need to find ways to show off all our accomplishments, even when they don't represent who or what we truly are. It's just ego saying, "I'm here! Look at me."

I don't know if you pay much attention to your dream life. Most folks don't. This makes me curious. Why do we ignore something that we spend much of our sleep cycle doing? Six years of our life by most averaged explanations. Why would God have made this a part of our every night experience for no apparent reason at all? Or, does he at times speak to us in this way, and we ignore it because it doesn't fit our scientific or faith paradigm? The ancients didn't ignore it.

Joseph had a couple of dreams. Like most dreams, they were pretty weird. That's probably why we ignore them so much, because it would be hard to make any sense of them. Joseph also had a special gift. Not only did he have meaningful dreams, but he could also understand the message they were trying to get across.

The first dream had to do with bundles of grain his brothers were working with bowing down to his bundle of grain. It doesn't take much dream interpretive skill to figure out where that one was going, but in case there was any confusion Joseph had a second dream. In this dream the sun, the moon, and eleven stars all got down on their knees and submitted to him. Hmmm! Let's see. Could that be Dad, Mom, and eleven brothers? Not even Dad was happy about this one, and Joseph's pride once again put him in the hot seat with his brothers.

Who with siblings hasn't fantasized about selling them off? It's rare that while you are fantasizing about such a thing a band of traders would be coming down the road. It turned out to be just such a day for the brothers. They sold Joseph. They tore his pretty coat into pieces, splashed some animal blood on it, and sent it back to Dad. Dad could only write one story about this, and it was that Joseph had been some wild animal's lunch. Meanwhile, Joseph was off to Egypt probably starting to question whether or not mentioning his dream out loud was a good idea.

In Egypt, bad matters just got worse. Joseph was sold to a guy with advanced military status. God was with him and he rose up through the household ranks rather fast. That is until the guy's wife came on to him, and in doing the right thing by turning her down, she claimed that he had made a rather violent pass at her. Now Joseph found himself in an Egyptian prison.

The good thing is that our egos cannot take us any place that God's love cannot go. God was here in prison with Joseph too, even as he was learning the hard knock lessons of becoming a human being. It wasn't long before Joseph was at the top of the heap in prison life. He was running the whole kit and caboodle. If you're going to be in prison, then it doesn't hurt to at least be in charge.

It turns out that the Pharaoh was rather discerning in his culinary taste. After being served a stale glass of wine and a dry piece of chocolate cake the Pharaoh's cup-bearer and chief baker found themselves keeping company with the country's criminal riffraff down with Joseph in a jail cell.

One morning Joseph noticed that these two guys looked a little down in the mouth. He asked them what was going on. They both mentioned that they had dreams the night before that they didn't understand, and the dreams were disturbing them. Wait a second. Isn't interrupting dreams how Joseph got himself into trouble the first time around? Can you imagine what these moments felt like when he was having to determine whether he should help these guys out or not? Or, maybe this was the first chance for his dream interpreting gift to be put to work for others and not for himself. Maybe this was an opportunity to turn weakness into strength.

Joseph inquired about the dreams and what ensued was a bunch of weirdness about the cup-bearer's grapevines and birds eating bread out of baskets on top of the baker's head. According to Joseph's interpretation the cup-bearer was going to be reinstalled to his original position and the baker was going to meet with a rather painful and humiliating execution at the hands of the Pharaoh. Joseph told the cup-bearer to remember him when he got his job back. The baker wasn't going to be much help.

Everything happened exactly as Joseph had predicted via the dreams. However, the cup-bearer forgot all about Joseph.

Two years passed before the Pharaoh himself would have a disturbing encounter with things that go bump in the night during dreamtime. At this point the cup-bearer remembered his old pal Joseph and told the Pharaoh that he might be able to help him out. Joseph was brought before Pharaoh, and told of dreams concerning seven scrawny cows eating seven fat ones and seven beautiful stocks of grain getting gobbled up by seven dried up shriveled ones. Joseph explained that this seemingly troubling dreamscape was in all actuality a gift by glimpse of things to come for the nation of Egypt. The number seven represented the number of years. There would be two sets of seven years. The first set of seven years represented a time of abundant harvest when the grain warehouses of the country would be bursting at the seams. The first seven years would be followed by the second seven years, and would be a time when drought and famine would descend upon the region. Good news followed by bad news.

Joesph took the opportunity to show off a few of the mad administrative skills that he had gained during his time as slave butler and jail administrator. He told the Pharaoh that he had a great idea.

Joseph said, "Hey Mr. Pharaoh, what if you took all the extra crops and grains that are going to grow over the course of the good seven years, built some silos, and stored them up so they would be around when we get to the seven years of famine. Everybody would be fed during the bad years and you would be a hero!"

What leader doesn't like an idea that makes them a hero?

Pharaoh replied, "Joseph, you seem to have a great head on your shoulders. That's a good idea. Why don't you make it happen? You are now second in command of all of Egypt only second to me."

As Joseph's dreams came to fruition, and his plan came to pass, he was eventually reunited with his family who had come from their own country in search of food during the famine. His original dreams came true too. His family would in fact bow before him, but now it would be a humbler version of Joseph. He had now become a human being.

Thanks for hanging with me. That was a long story. It was even longer for Joseph. From the time that his brothers sold him into slavery to the point where he became the second in command of the most powerful nation in the world was thirteen years. Thirteen years of questioning past decisions. Thirteen years of challenging and seemingly unfair circumstances. Thirteen years of being molded and shaped. Thirteen years of evolving from a human doing, who only used his gifts and abilities for his own good, to becoming a human being most interested in the wellbeing of others. It took a while. It wasn't easy. But eventually, Joseph's greatest weakness became his greatest strength.

I would imagine that if you would have been able to ask Joseph at the end of his life, he would not have wanted much to have been different. He probably would have said no to a different path. Wisdom aged over time often teaches the one on the journey that there was really no other path they could have taken that would have led them to the same resting place— the place of human being. We must go through what we must go through. We must decide what we must decide. We must break how we must break in order to become what we were originally created to be. No one wants to hear that. We all want to believe there is an easier way, a magic set of words or wand that we can wave to take us beyond the troubling parts of our path. There is not. All we can really do is keep walking until we recognize that we are surrounded by God's love in spite of our broken. Until like Joseph we can say with thankfulness, "Hi, my name is Joseph and I am a thankful and recovering…"

If being thankful for what's broken is still not making much sense, I understand. Hang with me a bit longer.

***

So how can we be truly thankful for the broken that has been a part of our lives? It hurts to be broken, whether it is self-inflicted, purposely done to us, or we are simply collateral damage. How can that brokenness be made into beauty?

The difficulty in relaying an idea through book form is that you the reader get the sense that when I wrote the last question, that I the writer had an amazing drop the mic answer already prepared that I was getting ready to throw down on you. Truth is I did not. After having written that question my laptop has lain dormant for days because I have felt I have nothing further to say on this matter. I have struggled with what the real answer is.

I did consider telling you stories of addicts who have gone to sleep in my comfortable, suburban church office floor while I spent the day woking to get them into a rehab facility. Or the numerous phone calls I get nowadays of someone telling me that they've got a friend or family member who they think is drinking too much or on something and wondering if there is anything I might share, or if I am willing to talk to them—I am always willing. There are quite a few amazing stories, and they all do highlight the fact that our greatest weakness can be turned into a strength that is beneficial to the world around us. However, the stories alone fall short of turning one's attitude to the place where we do not just accept the brokenness that is a part of life, but actually "all in" celebrate it. Brokenness cannot be turned into beauty unless the one looking at the brokenness sees it as beautiful. I guess this is where the old adage comes in, "Beauty is in the eye of the beholder."

This part of life is not about how we write fictional stories in our heads of what might occur, this is about how we interpret the stories of our life that have already been written. We all deal with our pain in different and interesting ways. Some of us stay in a state of denial that anything bad has ever happened to us, or denial that we are the actual culprit behind a few of the world's atrocities. Others of us know the world around us is a broken place and that we are partly to blame, but that just makes us angry and resentful, and due to our unwillingness to deal we propagate further pain and suffering upon ourselves and others. A few of us reach the point where we come to accept the broken in ourselves and others, and then just chug along accordingly taking in whatever more life has to throw our direction with little to no effort in shaping our stories, but just allowing them to become whatever they become. While these folks may achieve some level of peace, they're still missing out on another exciting and key component of a life well lived. Then there is the small sliver of the population who come to accept that they are broken, and they can see the broken all around them. They also see how the broken in their lives has shaped them. How it has helped them transform from a human doing into a human being. They recognize that without having experienced the brokenness within and without they would never have come to experience the thing that those who just accept life are missing. While some just have peace, they have come to experience real joy.

The people who can see beauty in the broken are also the people of hope. Who would not agree that we need a few more of those people in the world? They are the people who recognize the potential in the broken, because they can see what the broken has become in their own life. Every broken piece they encounter is viewed with a sense of potential. What can be done with that piece now? How can that piece be repurposed or rehabilitated into something of which not to be ashamed, but rather to be shown off?

***

Somewhere in all of my recovery reading I was introduced to the Japanese art of kintsuji. There was a time when everything one owned was not quite so disposable. The value of most things we posses today is so low that when it breaks we just throw it away and go get a new one. Even when it's not broken we trade the old in as soon as the newer version becomes available. Back in the day—barely over a century ago—things weren't massed produced. This made them not only rare, but more valuable. Even something as simple as a bowl to eat your morning Froot Loops from was a precious commodity. It was typically some form of carving or pottery made by a master craftsman. The value was often judged by who the craftsman was who had designed and shaped it. Should it get dropped while loading the ancient version of whatever a dishwasher was, then it was not so easy to replace. I'm sure many a kid lost afternoon samurai sword privileges over just such a mishap.

Broken or not, you don't just throw out the work of a master craftsman. Not only would it be a waste that you can't afford, but it would be rude to the maker. It may be hard to do, but you take it back to them and explain what happened. You then ask them what they can do to put it back together again.

In Japan, the craftsmen began to see this as a rare opportunity. An opportunity to take their original work, and turn it into something more than just a bowl for cereal. An opportunity to take the broken pieces of their work and repair them in such a way to where people wouldn't even want to use them for their original purpose anymore. An opportunity to create art for display. An opportunity to wow the owner and add even greater value to what they had already made so beautiful before. The bowl may have been broken, but the work of the artisan was not to go to waste. It would be improved upon and perfected.

In my house growing up Elmer's glue was the go-to fix-it adhesive of choice. Problem is, I can't think of too many works of art I ever produced as a result of my repair attempts. If you're going to make something more valuable, then what you use to repair it is of great importance. For Japanese craftsman their choice of sticky materials became melted liquid gold or silver. Now that will bring the stock value of pottery up a few bucks.

Each piece is slowly and methodically rejoined into its original position, yet this time it is going to be more brilliant. This time it is going to be given a strength that it did not have before, and uniqueness that will never again be replicated. What were once cracks that represented a place of destruction are now filled in with the indestructible strength of a precious metal. What used to be the pottery's place of greatest weakness has now become the point of its greatest strength. Not only are the cracks now strong, but the way they have been mended has brought the pathway of the piece's brokenness into greater awareness for the onlooker. These pathways are not marks of shame upon the pottery, they are now their places of greatest beauty and value.

Like the bowl of an ancient craftsman, each one of us starts out with a beautiful purpose and design. At some stage of our journey we decide it's not enough to just be the amazing that we have been created to be, and we determine we need to prove our value and worth. We become a human doing. In the process of doing and "making ourselves useful" we get hit, chipped, dropped, and broken along the way. Unfortunately, for much of humanity this is where real living ends. From this point forward shame, guilt, fear, resentment, and anger begin to be the driving forces of our daily arrangement. We cease to passionately create, inspire, and fiercely forge ahead. We retire from existence as human doings, and never deeply dive into the peace and joy that are offered to us in becoming human beings.

We don't have to stay broken though. We don't have to mind-numbingly continue to operate on the cruise control of human doing. We can stop the madness. We can be still. We can invite the Creator to pick up the pieces of our lives. The original Creator posses the indestructible adhesive of love that will not only bind our broken, but highlight the cracks of our messed up doing in such a way as to make them the most useful and beautiful things about us. Through our brokenness, mended by love, we can become a version of ourselves that is proud to be shown off, and satisfied to just be human.

***

The potential for beautiful art lies scattered all along the pathway of your life. Like most of us you have purposely walked right by some of the most valuable and potential packed pieces of your life's work, because in those pieces lie the pain. The pain of an alcoholic mom or dad, the pain of having been sexually abused or misused, the pain of spousal rejection and abandonment, the pain and shame of being the perpetrator in other's lives of the above named causes of pain, and the list of potential painful pieces goes on and on. Each of them are part of your life's greatest potential.

The masterpiece that is your life is not complete without their central role. It is time to pick up those pieces. It is time to quit being angry about them. It is time to quit being ashamed of them. It is time to not only to accept, but to actually celebrate them. It is time, like Joseph, to hand them to the God who is love, and let Him place them in the prominent position of your life that they belong. It's then your job to get out there and show off what they have become. The world desperately needs the work of art that is your life. It is time for your greatest weakness to become your greatest strength. It's time for you to be able to say your own proud version of:

"My name is John, and I'm a grateful and recovering alcoholic!"

Closing Thoughts:
Breathe Deep. Enjoy Now.

It had finally happened. I wasn't the worse case they had ever seen. I would not be spending the rest of my life behind the gates of a facility that had been designed to protect me from myself. After twenty-eight days the powers that be had come to believe that I had the necessary skills to be able to drive past the liquor store and walk past the airport bar without rushing to set a new Guinness World Record on drinks prior to total self destruction. I was free!

Now before we start cracking out bottles of champagne to celebrate—that would certainly not be an appropriate response considering this book's subject matter—let's get clear on exactly what I was free from. It's not addiction. I will always be a grateful and recovering alcoholic.

The way I like to view my alcoholism is that on a beautiful spring day one May, I was aided in pulling my alcoholism over and issuing an arrest warrant. On that day was the trial and jury verdict resulting in the incarceration of my alcoholism. Oddly enough God did not throw away the key to the jail cell. He had the audacity and trust to hand it to me for my own safe keeping. The God of love believes in me, just like he believes in you. He never takes away our choices. In fact, he is always expanding them to ever increasing possibility, in spite of the reality that he knows we will at times make the choice that hurts ourselves or others. The pottery would include no gold had it not been broken and repaired. Because He loves me he let me keep the key to my addiction.

***

While my addiction is locked away, it is always present within me. Like any hardened, long-term prisoner it is meticulously planning its escape. Doing push-ups, watching the patterns of how I guard the cell, and waiting for just the right moment to get me stressed or angry enough to let him out for just one little sip. My addiction is still real and present. But thankfully, up and until this moment of the day, he is on lock down. In fact, I very rarely even hear him say much anymore.

So if addiction is still around in some capacity, then what is it from which I feel so much freedom? The simple answer is human doing.

No longer do I feel trapped in a hollow cycle of identity building that doesn't include the organic substances that form me like love, creativity, and inspiration of others. There is no longer any compelling need to pursue anything that does not include these personal life essentials. The freedom to become a human being and regularly experience love, joy, and peace despite all the human doing around me that results in fear, resentment, and stress is the greatest gift that I have ever been given. Life's not perfect, but its way better spent Being rather than Doing.

***

It was hard to believe that so much could be different after only a hundred and twenty days. It was early fall and as I enjoyed a brisk outdoor walk through the neighborhood it felt as if nature's air conditioner had been set to the degree of perfect. Although I live sandwiched between two of the east coast's largest cities, the air I was breathing felt as fresh and clear as it would in the most uninhabited parts of the world. The birds had shown up in their formal wear and were putting on a concerto that even Beethoven could have heard and would have applauded in his deaf latter years.

Life was good. I was undergoing a complete and total personal transformation. I found myself in the gym three times a week, walking three miles most days, which included a lot of interaction with God, and not the type I had in the chapel at rehab. I had already lost the beer belly to the tune of twenty five pounds, and was regularly practicing stillness. I had not achieved perfection and was no longer looking for it. I had found something far better. Peace. The personal transformation was from human doing into a human being.

As I thankfully pondered the wonder of what was taking place in my life, I recognized how truly simple it had been to really begin living. It's as if I had spent those years of active addiction feeling like I was drowning. I splashed, kicked, and flailed in feeble attempts to grab a breath and stay alive. I was DOING every thing I thought to do. Finally, a group of loving people—human beings—came along side the river of my life where this dramatic drowning scene was playing out and began hollering the answers to me.

"John, stand up! John, just stand up!" they shouted.

At the last moment of air I heard their voices. I took the simple advice. I stood up. Much to my surprise I had only been in a few inches of water the whole time. I just discovered it was far more easy to BE than to DO.

It was on that walk that I knew my life would have to be devoted to this cause. The cause of helping others discover the simple practices that will help them stop the madness of human doing and join the ever growing population of those who are becoming human beings. Becoming who we were originally created to BE.

This book, along with our company and online community of Mastering Modern Life, are our first attempts to share with you what we are continuing to learn. We'd love to assist you along the way of your own journey, and we have developed many resources to do just that. I hope you have been inspired in your own journey toward Becoming Human, and I look forward to our continued journey together.

Until we meet again soon, don't forget to Breathe Deep and Enjoy Now.

About the Author

John was born with a Type AAA personality and boundless imagination, which sounds like the makings of a world-changing scenario, but in his case it culminated into a nine-year battle with alcoholism. The irony of his addiction is that it was seemingly at odds with his chosen profession. John has been serving in various church leadership roles in churches ranging from 35 to 22,000 in membership for the past 25 years. While he was well seasoned in guiding others he had not yet found how to walk the path of his own life with joy. Then he experienced 120 days that would forever transform his way of approaching the journey of life. A few simple practices put into action would bring him to discover that the amazing life he was looking for was the one he had always been living, and that there was even more available on this incredible expedition. Through this experience, he discovered the transformational journey of Becoming Human. Now, along with serving as the Executive Pastor of The Church at Severn Run, loving life with Mrs. Amazing—Amber, and raising his three Crazies, John is in a passionate pursuit to discover and develop simple practices to help others undergo a lifestyle transformation that will help them to Breath Deep and Enjoy Now. He works with his high powered team at the company he founded, Mastering Modern Life, to deliver these simple practices through a variety of avenues with his spiritually sarcastic, down to earth, storytelling style. He wants the world to Breathe Deep and Enjoy Now!

More About
Mastering Modern Life:

 Change can be hard to accomplish by yourself. That's why you need others devoted to helping you achieve the lifestyle transformation the True You desires. We at Mastering Modern Life are devoted to being that team you need to live the life you have always dreamed about. Whether you are looking to achieve more in the way of relationships, health, career, finances, or just general happiness, we have the experience, pathway, tools and most importantly the encouragement you need to start your journey toward the amazing next. We would love to join you on your journey! Find out more at MasteringModernLife.com and follow us on Facebook, Instagram, and YouTube.